What Others Are Saying About Lasting Impressions

"Style. Creativity. Gimmicks. These can generate a certain buzz and attract people to your church. But when style trumps substance, creativity wins over content, and gimmicks overshadow real growth, we've missed the mark. Mark's insight in this book on connecting people with God and others in real and lasting ways is right on. He reminds us again that *everyone* matters to God, and, because of that, we need to meet people where they are—not where we wish they were. Getting them in the front door is one thing. Keeping them from going out the back door is quite another. Pastor, read this book and remember again why we all got into this thing called church in the first place!"

Ed Young
Senior Pastor, Fellowship Church
Author of *The Creative Leader*

"Waltz says it clearly: You can't make people change—that's God's job. However, the local church *can* create space that is conducive to the work of the Holy Spirit in people's lives. Want people to do more than visit your church? Read *Lasting Impressions*, wrestle with what is and what could be, then develop or redevelop your plan to help people belong—to God and each other."

Craig Groschel
Senior Pastor, LifeChurch.tv
Author of *IT: How Churches and Leaders Can Get It and Keep It.*

"I loved Mark's first book, *First Impressions*. And *Lasting Impressions* takes it a step further. Every leader who is serious about getting people connected to their church needs to read this book. Inspirational and practical."

Mark Batterson
Lead Pastor, National Community Church, Washington, D.C.
Author of *In a Pit with a Lion on a Snowy Day* and
Wild Goose Chase

"We serve a 'going-out God' who meets us where we are. This book reflects his heart. It will help you to go out to people visiting your church and meet them at their point of need…and keep them coming back for more! Mark Waltz and the entire staff at Granger Community Church have much to teach us (more specifically, me) about reaching those who aren't in church because they feel unworthy, unloved, and unlovable."

Dr. Joel C. Hunter
Senior Pastor, Northland: A Church Distributed

"In this practical piece, Mark rolls up his sleeves and digs deep, unafraid of getting dirty with what Jesus truly meant by loving people. Seasoned with stories and illustrations from Granger's cutting-edge methodology of ministry, readers will walk away with both conviction and courage for applying these principles within their context."

Kary Oberbrunner, "recovering Pharisee" and
Author of *The Fine Line*

LASTING IMPRESSIONS

FROM **VISITING** TO **BELONGING**

MARK WALTZ

Loveland, Colorado
group.com

Group resources really work!

This Group resource incorporates our R.E.A.L. approach to ministry. It reinforces a growing friendship with Jesus, encourages long-term learning, and results in life transformation, because it's:

Relational—Learner-to-learner interaction enhances learning and builds Christian friendships.

Experiential—What learners experience through discussion and action sticks with them up to 9 times longer than what they simply hear or read.

Applicable—The aim of Christian education is to equip learners to be both hearers and doers of God's Word.

Learner-based—Learners understand and retain more when the learning process takes into consideration how they learn best.

Lasting Impressions: From Visiting to Belonging
Copyright © 2013 Mark L. Waltz

Visit our website | group.com

ISBN 978-0-7644-9108-5
Printed in the United States of America.
10 9 8 7 6 5 4 3 2 1   18 17 16 15 14 13

Dedication

To Mark Beeson, founding and senior pastor of Granger Community Church. This book is the result of your vision to reach people with the good news that they matter to God. For more than 25 years, you have been about helping people take their next steps toward Christ…together. That's been your mission at Granger since 1986 when you and your family moved to northern Indiana to pioneer a new approach to ministry in the local church. You're always asking, "What's your next step?"

And since *everyone* has a next step, you've led the way by leaning into your own next step. Thank you for modeling this norm. And for allowing me to do life with you, for allowing me to hear the tension you feel, to see the challenges you face, and to experience the courage you find to take your next step. Your modeling reminds me that the title "pastor" next to my name doesn't eliminate my need to grow, to take my next step. There is always a next one.

Thank you for taking such a genuine interest in my family and in my personal journey. Your cheerleading has encouraged me to be faithful with my steps. You are my good friend, even as I respect you as my boss. Thank you for trusting me to lead beside you. Your vision is my vision now. And we share it with thousands whose lives are being transformed by the grace and power of Jesus Christ.

With tremendous gratitude I dedicate this work to you.

Acknowledgments

My next steps have always been taken in the context of relationship (and so have yours). My journey has been more enjoyable and fulfilling because it's been shared with people. People who extend grace when I stumble. People who help by listening and processing with me. People who share my passion to see others experience God's purpose for their lives by taking their next steps toward him.

- Laura, my best friend, my lover, and my life partner, you are a faithful sojourner. You've patiently accepted my erratic schedule and the glow of my laptop screen well into the early morning hours. You've been my sounding board, my cheerleader, and my truth-teller. I experience the character of God in your grace. Thank you for sharing life with me, all of it. You are a true gift from God.

- Olivia, although you'll always be my "baby girl," you've already grown to be quite the young lady. I love your curiosity about life and your love for people. You are mature beyond your years, and I couldn't be prouder to be your dad.

- Tim Stevens, your friendship has marked my life. Your leadership has inspired me. You challenge me to lead from my own unique style, you care about my marriage and family, and you share my warped sense of humor. Thank you for your trust.

- Rob Wegner, Jason Miller, and Kem Meyer, my friends who round out the senior management team at Granger, what a ride! You challenge me, encourage me, and laugh hard with me. I love sharing this journey with you!

- Julie Smies, as my administrative assistant, you understand what it is to be an advocate. You represent me, organize me, cheerlead me, and, along with my wife, help me look better than I really am.

- Nylee Gatling, Dawn Lovitt, Kim Volheim, and Gene Troyer—what a team! Your collaborative efforts to help people take steps toward Christ in relationships with others are unparalleled.

- To my editor, Bob D'Ambrosio, and the team at Group Publishing, thank you for your trust and partnership in resourcing the church.

Contents

Foreword

When I read Mark's work, I think about the word *impression*. As in, you never get a second chance to make a first one. Often the word is used in our culture in superficial ways. We all suffer from wanting to impress people. We often engage in what is sometimes called impression management—trying to manipulate the way others think of us.

But there is—or can be—something deeper going on. An impression can also be the deep and lasting mark that is made by a powerful encounter. Like the impression a seal makes in wax, much as we are to be sealed in the Spirit. Like the way other people make an impression on us when our minds are taught to think in new ways and never quite return to their original shapes.

Churches are to be places of impression. But that doesn't mean they're to be places where we try to get people to say "Wow!" at the cleverness of our talks or the slickness of our organizations. (On the other hand, they're not meant to be places where people say "Wow!" at the insipid blandness of our talks or at the level of our disorganization.)

There's another impression that God is interested in, and that's the impression the Holy Spirit can make on a human heart. When someone is convicted of sin and repents, when someone is guided into a whole new level of servanthood, when someone is awakened to the palpable presence of God, when someone who has been alone or rejected discovers a community where he or she is embraced and included, then the lasting impression has begun.

Mark and the team he works with at Granger are giving some of the best thought in our day to the idea of lasting impressions in the church. Here he lays out a vision of church as a place where people discover they can belong and become what they never dreamed. A vision where the voice of the Spirit can be heard in new and fresh ways by people who thought they were spiritually tone-deaf. It's a vision that might change you, your church, and people who don't even know God right now.

Read it, and be impressed.

John Ortberg, Senior Pastor
Menlo Park Presbyterian Church
Menlo Park, California

Introduction

New people visit your church. And that's a big deal.

Then they return for a second visit. That's an even bigger deal.

They come for a variety of reasons. Some show up to quiet an insistent spouse. Others decide to visit because they've heard about the children's center, the youth program, the worship band, or the new message series. Still others attend because they are at the end of their ropes. They have nowhere else to turn. Ultimately, most of the people new to your church have one thing in common: They are looking for help, for hope.

They also show up with the mind-set of a consumer, naturally wondering, "What's in it for me?" So you meet them right where they are. You create a welcoming and safe environment for them. You treat them as if they matter. And they do. They matter to God, and therefore they matter to you and your church. The message begins to soak in. They *do* matter.

I think first impressions are so important that I wrote a book about them: *First Impressions: Creating Wow Experiences in Your Church* (Group Publishing, Inc., 2013). In it, I describe ways to ensure that first-time visitors get the message that they matter to you and everyone in your church. But what about visitors who continue to attend your church but don't yet feel a sense of belonging? How do you help them engage further in your church? How do you encourage them to connect—with God, with other people, with the ministry and mission of your church? How do you help them move from being hopeful consumers to other-focused, step-taking, involved participants? In short, how does your church move people from visiting to belonging?

The answer to that question is a bigger deal than a guest's first or second visit to your church. Helping people experience the reality of belonging— to God and others—in a way that causes them to live *for* God and others is kingdom-of-God-sized stuff. That's a really big deal.

This book will not only explore a biblical philosophy for helping people take steps toward Christ, but will also offer realistic, doable steps to create a culture where taking steps is normal and normal people take steps. I've learned that this culture is cultivated when we create environments and make space for experiences that are intuitively understood and easily accessed.

This book will help you

- identify what is your responsibility in that process and what isn't.
- develop experiences that encourage people to explore, discover, and grow in their personal journeys toward and with Christ.
- understand the value of organic relationship.
- honor God as you offer your best to your people and community.

Throughout the book, you'll find references to Granger Community Church, where I lead our connections and multisite ministries. As of this writing, our Granger campus gathers thousands each weekend. Our congregation in Elkhart is made up of nearly 500 people. We've just launched our third site in La Porte, Indiana, with several hundred attending. Everything here has direct application to each of our venues. I offer these references to our ministry approach as illustrations. I've also included ministry examples from other churches to encourage you to explore a variety of methods to accomplish the same outcome: involving people who are sticking around your church, wondering what's next. Your approach will be unique because your church is unique. But regardless of size, the principles are transferable.

You'll find exercises sprinkled throughout the book, as well as review questions at the end of each chapter. Consider them privately, or use them to spark conversation among your board or team. I've included some work sheets that may be helpful in structuring, training, and evaluating your teams. Feel free to revise them to best fit your ministry culture. Use this book as a guide to help you tap the resources God has already planted within your church.

I trust your goal is the same as ours at Granger. We want to see people hang around the church long enough to experience how much they matter to God—and then extend that reality to the people around them. We want them to move from feeling "it's all about me" to "it's not about me—it's about others."

People matter right where they are. But they matter too much to leave them there. Now *that's* a big deal.

Mark Waltz
Granger, IN

People Still Matter

"Acceptance is an act of the heart. To accept someone is to affirm to them that you think it's a very good thing they are alive."
—John Ortberg[1]

Playing Peekaboo

When our daughter, Olivia, was a baby, she and I played Peekaboo. I'd fan her blankie slowly across her face, asking in a high-pitched, melodic voice, "Where's Olivia?" And as the blanket cleared her face, her little eyes would widen with delight, her face would light up with the biggest, brightest grin, and I would be treated to the sweet sound of her infant laugh.

As time passed, Olivia began to initiate the game. She would cover her eyes with her tiny hands, and I would ask, "Where's Olivia?" Now the element of surprise was in her hands. With the same heart-gripping laugh, she would fling her hands to the side, revealing that she was, indeed, "right here!"

I knew where Olivia was. And so did she, although she pretended to be "somewhere else." Sounds like a familiar scene from Genesis 3, doesn't it? "But the Lord God called to the man, 'Where are you?' He answered, 'I heard you in the garden, and I was afraid because I was naked; so I hid' " (Genesis 3:9-10).

This time the players in the game of Peekaboo are God and Adam. Adam doesn't have his fig-leaf blankie yet, so he improvises by standing behind some tall shrubs. God's the one asking, "Where's Adam?"

God knew where Adam was, as surely as I knew where Olivia was. Even so, God asked, "Adam, where are you?"

I'm not the first person to consider the profound theological meaning of this scene. Here's the point I want to explore with you: God met Adam right where he was. Period.

Maybe Adam longed to be somewhere—anywhere—besides standing buck naked behind a shrub. Maybe Olivia actually wished she could be somewhere other than strapped into a baby swing. But, as reality would have it, Olivia was right in front of me. And Adam was standing in front of God.

I knew it. Olivia couldn't be anywhere but where she was.

God knew it. Adam couldn't be anywhere but where he was.

And our guests, our attendees, our members—our people—can't be anywhere but where they are.

OK, not so profound. But it is critically important.

My uncle may wish he didn't smoke, but he does. Your boss may wish she weren't so controlling, but, alas, she is. And as I write this chapter, I may wish this book were further along, but it isn't.

We are where we are. We must accept that fact about ourselves, and we must accept that fact about others.

Vision vs. Veracity

We know that people don't have to stay where they are. My uncle doesn't have to be a smoker next year. Your boss may not be so controlling tomorrow (but probably will be). I will have finished this book because you're now reading it. People can move from where they are. It is possible.

But our temptation is to rush people along. We want to help them get through their current situations or life stages—now. We know what's possible. We know the reality that can be their lives. But when we jump too quickly to a hope that isn't yet reality, we shortcut the opportunity to extend grace. Acceptance that conveys, "I will accept you when…" isn't acceptance. We extend grace when our acceptance comes without requirements. It's unconditional. It's not dependent on what's possible tomorrow. Grace is today, regardless.

> We extend grace when our acceptance comes without requirements. It's unconditional. It's not dependent on what's possible tomorrow. Grace is today, regardless.

There's certainly something to be said for speaking vision into the lives of others, pointing them to a promising future. There is a place for such Spirit-driven, possibility-charged encouragement. But such vision must have a starting place.

When I visit a city, I often wander into a mall to pick up a memento for my wife or daughter. If I know the kind of store I want to find—a clothing store, music store, novelty store—I look first for the mall directory.

I have a clear vision. I know what I'm looking for. I've already pictured the kind of thing I want to carry out of the mall when I leave. So I look for the store most likely to sell that product. But I look for another marker on the mall directory. I look for the "x" or the arrow that says, "You are here." I could wander the mall and eventually find the store I've envisioned, but I will find it more quickly if I first identify where I am.

Even though I want to be in that store, I'm not. I'm here. Right here where the "x" says I am. I have to start here—at the "x." Then, and only then, can I chart a path that will get me from veracity—what is real—to my vision, where I want to be.

At Granger we decided a long time ago to simply meet people where they are. I addressed this in my first book, *First Impressions*: "At Granger, [our] mission is 'helping people take their next step toward Christ…together.' This motivates us to create a safe and welcoming environment for our guests. [Our mission] drives us to meet people where they are, not where we wish they were."[2]

Here's the catch: When people are no longer "new," we often change our expectations of them. We somehow expect that because they've been around our church for a few weeks or months, they're suddenly at some new reality, some new "x," in their story lines.

What Does Being in Church Mean About Being in Church?

I'm convinced that many churches reach some unevaluated, even subconscious, conclusions about people who have recently begun attending church regularly. Which of the following do you expect of people who have attended your church for, say, three months?

- They've heard enough teaching to enable them to kick a filthy habit.

- He should be moving out of his girlfriend's apartment.

- She should be tithing by now.

- They should be reading the Bible daily and discussing it in a small group or Bible study.

- She must understand why that blouse is inappropriate for church.

Often these assumptions and expectations reflect a narrow vision the church has for her people. Believing what we see for them as the *best* reality, we suspend celebrating until they've demonstrated behavior that is acceptable in the church's eyes. That's not vision. That's judgment.

> Believing what we see for them as the *best* reality, we suspend celebrating until they've demonstrated behavior that is acceptable in the church's eyes.

At Granger there are people serving on our traffic teams who are still fighting overwhelming addictions. There are women in Bible studies who don't know how to love their kids in a healthy way. There are men serving in technical arts who aren't convinced Jesus is who he claims to be. Every weekend people who are cheating on their spouses, their taxes, or their sales reports return to a service to hear how much they matter to God.

They are where they are.

And we must meet them there.

Rather than merely expecting people to "get it," we must think in terms of journey, one step at a time. What steps will she take to get out of an illicit affair? What will he experience before the addiction is under control? What next move will ultimately lead him to a life-redeeming, personal relationship with Jesus?

That step will require someone to say, "Peekaboo. I see where you are. Under the blankie, buck naked behind the tree. And I'm not requiring you to be anywhere else. I love you and accept you right now, right here."

God knew where Adam was. Even so, he asked Adam, "Where are you?" He knew *Adam needed to acknowledge where he was*. Adam could have continued to hide. He could have dreamed about being free from this new experience of shame. But all the dreaming about what could be would not make the "could be" a reality. He had to say, "I'm right here. Yeah, I'm naked behind the tree."

Then Adam would discover two truths that our people must experience within our churches. First, God was still there. He didn't wait to show up until Adam and Eve had worked up an apology letter. He didn't wait until Adam had made his own environmentally friendly, three-button fig-leaf evening coat. He accepted Adam right where he was.

Second, Adam then had clarity about what was next. Because he acknowledged, "I'm here," the next step was clear. He had to come out of hiding—something he couldn't have done if he hadn't first admitted he was hiding.

People can only be where they are—even after being around your church for a while, even after they aren't "new."

The Problem With Being "Not New"

Almost everyone has been one of the "new people." And we like it. Perhaps you've been one of the new people...

- when you got the new-customer phone pricing with your cell phone company.

- at a restaurant you've visited for the first time.

- with a special introductory interest rate on a new credit card.

- in a frequent-flyer program.

- as a bank customer.

- when you subscribed to a magazine for the first time.

I've been one of the new people on a number of occasions. For example, I've subscribed as a paying customer to four different cell phone companies over the past few years. Without exception each company courted me with special offers: free phones; additional services for an introductory period; or upgraded, full-feature phones for a fraction of the retail cost. Just for signing up (yes, with a two-year binding contract). All for me because I was new. It felt good to be one of the new people.

Each time I made a contractual agreement, living, kind people were available to help me understand the phone I'd selected, set up my new account, and answer my questions. "This company cares about me!" I thought.

And then (sooner rather than later) I wasn't new anymore. I was *just* a customer. A contractually bound customer. Crud.

No more free phones, free music downloads, free text messaging, or free web browsing. I wasn't *new*.

I've noticed that we tend to treat inanimate objects in much the same manner. Many of us tend to treat things—from cars to tennis shoes—better when they're still new. We wash a new car every few days and avoid getting dirt on our new shoes. But give that car or pair of shoes a few months, and our attentiveness subsides. We wash the car less often and stop being so guarded with our tennies. We treat them differently.

Here's what I know. The value of a cell phone, a pair of shoes, or an automobile depreciates over time. But people are human beings created by God. And what was true about them when they were new is still true today. They matter. They have intrinsic, God-given worth. And they are where they are: whether it's their first week, first month, or 27th visit.

Getting Real About Where People Really Are

A young woman—I'll call her Becky (although that's not her real name)—sent this note through our church website:

"Gosh, I really don't know what to say except I think I need to start coming to your church, but I'm scared. I'm going through a divorce right now and could really use some help from some positive and loving people. I haven't been to church in probably 20 years (I'm 28), but I was driving by GCC the other day, and something was telling me I should stop in, but I didn't. I really don't know what to do from here. Please help me!"

Within a few weeks, Becky had exuberantly announced to others that she was "regularly" attending our church. During those first few weeks, I don't know if her lifestyle was different. I don't know if she quickly followed Jesus as her boss. I do know she stepped into a Turning Point group we were offering at that time—a group journey designed to help people working on broken relationships, damaging styles of relating, or addictive behaviors. I do know that newfound friends at our church met Becky where she was—*and* they found a new friend in her.

Unfortunate scenarios unfold when churches fail to meet people where they are. See if you relate to any of the following.

Before Becky walked through the door of the church, someone from First Church e-mailed her four steps to salvation along with an offer to help her pray the sinner's prayer. Becky was confused. She didn't feel listened to, which meant she didn't feel cared for either. She didn't understand why she felt so guilty as she read the e-mail. After all, she didn't want the divorce; she just wanted help, as her e-mail had stated.

Or consider the approach Metro Community took. During Becky's second weekend experience, she was asked to join the LifeBuilders Sunday school class, a group of married couples. If that wasn't enough, they were studying the teachings of Jesus and Paul regarding marriage and divorce. Again, no one met her where she was.

Finally across town, Second City Memorial asked her to sing in the choir, teach a children's class, and make hospital visitations with Deacon Ralph and his wife. She didn't return. Small wonder.

Perhaps all of this sounds mildly far fetched. But is it?

Becky is in church. But just because she's there doesn't mean she's got everything figured out. And it certainly doesn't mean she has Jesus figured out. Will your church accept her where she is, or will your church require her to adopt the lifestyle, have the knowledge base, and be involved in church to the same degree that your Christ-followers are—now? I hope not.

Will anyone ask, "Becky, where are you?" The only place she can be today is where she is. Let's stop playing Peekaboo and meet our people right where they are. Wherever they are.

The fact is, everyone is at a different X. And they matter right there.

Right Where We Are, We Matter

Elaine (not her real name) had been attending Granger for about a year, and in that time had committed to following Jesus, had been baptized, and was serving on a volunteer team. Since that first connection when she understood how much she mattered to God, she had faithfully attended, sitting in the fifth row in the center section of the auditorium. She was home. She mattered to God.

One Sunday morning Elaine arrived late for the weekend service—not her norm. She got her children squared away in the children's center and then made her way to the service, which was already in progress. Realizing her fifth-row, center-section seat was occupied, she stood at the back of the room near a staff member from my team. She stood quietly and surveyed the room filled with a variety of people: young and old; seekers and followers; married, divorced, and single; rich and not-so-rich. After a few moments, she leaned over and whispered, "This is the first time I've had this view of the room. I knew I mattered to God, but standing here makes me realize that all these people matter to him, too."

Yes!

As much as I want people to understand they matter to God, the breakthrough revelation that catapults spiritual growth and a partnership in Christ's kingdom is this revelation: *Other* people matter to God. Right where they are.

And they must matter to us. Every person at the core of your church must get this. People matter. *Other* people matter. Other people *still* matter.

Period.

The breakthrough revelation that catapults spiritual growth and a partnership in Christ's kingdom is this revelation: *Other* people matter to God. Right where they are.

From Chapter 1

Your Local Church

■ When is a person no longer "new" at your church? How do expectations change once a person is not new?

■ Consider the three fictional churches that responded to Becky's e-mail. Which church is yours most like: First Church, with its four steps to salvation? Metro Community, with its Sunday school agenda? Second City Memorial, with its medley of volunteer expectations? Or is there a fourth option that better describes how your church connects with people where they are?

Your Personal Life

■ Consider your own journey. What were some of your recent steps toward Christ? Were other people aware of your next step before you recognized it? How much time passed before you actually took that step? What was the role of friends and other positive influences in your life? How did they communicate vision while you were at the "you are here" spot?

■ Make a short list of the people you know who still have an "obvious" step to take from where they are right now. Where do you wish they were on their journeys? How do you feel about their progress or lack of progress? How much time is enough before they take their next steps? When is your expectation an expression of grace? When is your expectation a pronouncement of judgment? When is your expectation a demonstration of accountability? How could you communicate vision to any of these people?

Endnotes

1. John Ortberg, *Everybody's Normal Till You Get to Know Them* (Grand Rapids, MI: Zondervan, 2003), 101.

2. Mark L. Waltz, *First Impressions: Creating Wow Experiences in Your Church* (Loveland, CO: Group Publishing, Inc., 2005), 29.

Assimilation: Watch Your Language

"People are not looking to experience sameness— the product of a program that sends each person through a step-by-step assembly line of so-called belonging."
—*Joseph R. Myers*[1]

I'm Not Buying

Years ago when my wife and I were starry-eyed newlyweds, we accepted an offer to tour a time-share vacation option. We had no money. We had no interest in a time share. But we did have a little time. How tough could it be to sit through a little presentation in return for one of several great gifts?

The presenter droned on and on. We began to realize we didn't have *that* much time. Finally his spiel was over. We were ready to decline the offer and claim our prize. But no. Not so fast.

We naively waited our turn to sit at a folding table with sales guy number 37. He, too, had a spiel. And lots of paper. Our eyes glazed over, and our ears ached from his jabber. Finally came the yes-or-no question. We were ready. "No," we said.

He wasn't. Not for that answer. He pressed. He spun. When he realized he couldn't persuade us, he asked us to wait while he called his manager over to sign off on our form. The manager was the initial spielmeister who had given the earlier impassioned sales pitch.

His pressure tactics were the same as our salesman's, but he was even more determined. When he finally relented, the two cutthroats sneered and sighed and pointed us to the prize center. The three-piece nylon luggage set did nothing to lift our spirits. We grabbed the burgundy wannabe bags and ran to the car.

We weren't buying. Not today. Not ever.

We would not be assimilated.

Have you experienced that kind of pressure? on a car lot? at your own front door with a door-to-door salesman? at church?

People Want to Be Treated With Respect

Whether the push and shove to "buy" is in a car dealership, a time-share meeting room, or the local church, people want to be treated with respect. We want interaction with other human beings who acknowledge that we are thinking adults with the ability to say yes or no based on our desires and needs. We feel disrespected, even insulted, when we are coerced.

No self-respecting adult wants to be parented. Even at church. Perhaps especially at church. When our program-driven agenda becomes more important than meeting people where they are, we risk sounding like the nagging parent: "You need to do this." "Stop doing that." "Complete this now." "Are you finished yet?"

We can easily make our approach—our programs, services, classes, and groups—more important than the people we hope to help.

But the truth is, we in the church *do* have an agenda. We want people to meet Jesus. We want people to experience the joy of living their lives caught up in the kingdom of God. But we can easily make our approach—our programs, services, classes, and groups—more important than the people we hope to help. When we do, people feel disrespected, insulted, and parented.

"I Don't Even Know You"

My wife, Laura, and I still date. We want to build into each other, so we prioritize time to talk, learn, and grow together. Besides all that, we love the romance, and dating keeps the flame going. I digress.

An evening date for us usually includes dining out, and deciding where we eat often falls to me. One evening I decided to take Laura to one of those Japanese restaurants where they prepare your meal right at your table. We'd never been there, but we'd talked about it often. Looking forward to the new experience, I opened the restaurant door for my wife…and stopped.

This was not what I expected. Every table in the restaurant seated eight, and every table was filled. I realized that meant we would be sitting at a table with strangers. Not exactly the intimate dinner for two we had in mind. I opened the door for Laura again, and we left. I love new adventures, but I generally want to know and trust the people I share them with.

We'll explore this more in Chapter 5, but for now, make a note: Most people need time to meet others, connect, and develop trust before they join us or share our agenda.

"I'm Fearful"

Tyler and Bev (fake names, true story) began their journey at Granger as a lot of people do: during the holidays, two visits in two years. Then they began to attend more frequently. They had trusted friends at Granger; otherwise, they probably wouldn't have attended to begin with. Over time the regularity of their visits increased, but their commitment didn't—not formally, anyway.

They found the messages informative and inspiring. They loved what the church was doing in the community. They even joined their friends in large-group volunteering opportunities. But they didn't step toward membership. Not right away. Not yet.

They were afraid. Afraid of obligatory requirements. Afraid they'd suddenly turn into freakishly hard-core radicals. Jesus freaks.

> I don't believe most people show up at your church or mine thinking, "Maybe this church has a great program or initiative into which I can selflessly pour myself."

And that's OK. Lots of people have been badly burned by the church. They may have felt condemned every time they walked into the church building. They may have felt they never measured up: Their clothes weren't right; their hair was too weird; their piercings were too numerous; their language wasn't refined. They never belonged. They just didn't fit.

So, hoping for a different experience, they come to your church; but they're reserved, afraid it will be church as usual. They're fearful.

Even committed Christ-followers are often afraid. Some of them have shown up in your church because the only way they knew how to step out of their serving roles at their last churches was to leave. They're testy. They're not jumping in too quickly. They're not saying yes to anything just yet. They need time.

"I Have an Agenda, Too"

I don't believe most people show up at your church or mine thinking, "Maybe this church has a great program or initiative into which I can selflessly pour myself." Most people who check out our churches are asking, "What's here for me?"

"Will this place help me raise my kids?"

"Can I find hope for my marriage here?"

"Will I ever crawl out of the rut I'm in?"

"Is this a safe place that will help me heal?"

These people don't want to be assimilated. Initially they may not care about our membership covenants, our small groups, or our Sunday school classes. What they do care about is whether we can help them address the issues right in front of them—the stuff that's affecting their quality of life, their sense of purpose and fulfillment.

Is it wrong to care about our returning guests' needs and desires? By doing so, are we just catering to their consumer mindsets? Is there a point during their second or third or fourth visit when we should say, "OK, we met you where you were. We recognize that your issues matter—to a point. Now it's time to buy into our agenda. Don't keep taking up a seat without making a contribution."

I don't know of any church that intentionally conveys this message, but we send it anyway if we pressure people to join our next level of "church club activities." If people matter to God, if people matter to us, then we must treat them as people—people created by the same Creator, bearing God's image, and expecting to be treated accordingly.

Beware the Agenda of Activity

Mere assimilation into a checklist of programs and activities seldom changes people. In 2007, Willow Creek Community Church conducted a survey of its congregation and those of 10 other churches of varying size and structure. The survey revealed that respondents had often mistaken their involvement in meetings, programs, and activities as indicators of their spiritual growth rather than approaches or environments that might *lead* to real-life transformation.[2] Getting people into our classes, groups, and gatherings isn't the point. However, if we build spaces and opportunities that encourage steps toward Christ, people might actually own their journeys and experience the wonder of spiritual transformation.

So even if we approach this with proper motives, how do we—the local church—live out our agenda, even promote our agenda, without pressuring our returning guests before they are ready to join us? We may experience little difficulty connecting people who come to our church as Christ-followers with former church backgrounds; the challenge is most often connecting new people with little or no church background who are still on a journey toward Christ.

Part of this challenge has been created by the church itself. Generations, even centuries, of taking steps away from what Jesus originally intended for his followers—an organic, relational partnership in the kingdom of heaven—has resulted in a widely shared perspective of organized religion that causes people to tune out invitations to find God in a church.

Institutionalized Church

Sometimes I like to wander into an out-of-the-way, mom-and-pop coffeehouse where the furnishings don't match, the dog-eared newspapers invite the next patron to browse, and the beverage menu doesn't match the selection found worldwide in the institutionalized mother of coffee shops. For years, one of my favorite local coffee shops was also favored by students from a nearby college. Although I like the consistency of Starbucks (a caramel macchiato is always a caramel macchiato), the smaller, independent java shops appeal to me because they're unique.

Generation X and Millennials increasingly feel a similar discontent with the institutionalized local church. I have friends in these life stages. They're good people. They love Jesus, and they love the body of Christ, but some of them bristle at the notion of membership. Denominations and megachurches make them uneasy. Some are apprehensive about organized churches with physical meeting spaces of any kind. Generally I hear them express

- a desire for organic, uncontrived, and honest relationships;

- discontentment with an inwardly focused, self-preserving agenda; and

- a longing to be part of a movement rather than a static establishment.

I couldn't agree more. I, too, want to be part of a movement of people, journeying together in authentic relationships, sharing a God-sized mission to bring the kingdom of heaven into our communities and the world in the here and now.

Resistance to church membership is not limited to any one life stage or age group. Pastors and priests who abused children, church leaders who embezzled or misappropriated funds, pastors who forfeited their leadership roles in return for illicit sex have given our society all the reasons it needs not to trust us. Decent, caring, responsible, thinking adults of all ages are leery of pledging their loyalty to the church through membership—for good reason.

Remember Tyler and Bev—the couple that resists church membership? They actually love what's going on at Granger. At their own level of safe involvement, they're part of it. But they don't want to "join." For them, membership brings a set of expectations that they don't necessarily disagree with, but it threatens to make what should be natural and organic somehow obligatory and forced.

Structure and the Institution

You can pick up dozens of books dealing with organizational leadership, structure, and management. My intent here is not to argue the need for structure in the local church. Suffice it to say, nothing of value ever happened without vision. And every vision that was ever realized did so because of a plan. The very nature of a plan implies organization and leadership.

> If "organic" is to be understood as lacking structure, then "organic" will never produce a vision nor the means to accomplish it.

If "organic" is to be understood as lacking structure, then "organic" will never produce a vision nor the means to accomplish it. But there's nothing more organic than the way Jesus paints the kingdom of God, *and* he has a plan to accomplish it. *We* are the plan. You and I. Your church, my church. We're the plan. We're the organic material. And we need mighty forces—the local church—all over the world to effectively implement a structured, strategic plan to join God in his work.

Invite People to a Movement

Jesus never invited anyone to club membership or an institution. When he called his disciples to follow him, he didn't initiate them with fraternity rites of passage or give them special privileges. When Jesus says that he's the only way to the Father (John 14:6), he isn't setting up First Church. Teacher and author Rob Bell notes that Jesus "was saying that his way, his words, his life is our connection to how things truly are at the deepest levels of existence. For Jesus then, the point of religion is to help us connect with ultimate reality, God." [3]

Jesus calls us to a movement, to live as citizens of the kingdom of God who love God with all our heart, mind, soul, and strength and to love our neighbors as ourselves (Mark 12:30-31). If people are merely called to membership, we are simply asking them to join an organization. It might be a "successful" organization, but it's institutionalized religion nonetheless.

> **W**e are not helping people convert to our culture; we are helping them convert to Christ."

At Granger we call people to join a movement. Our senior pastor, Mark Beeson, put it this way at a weekly staff meeting: "We are not helping people convert to our culture; we are helping them convert to Christ."

People want to belong to something bigger than they are, something exciting and adventurous, something excellent and significant. But if we aren't clear about calling people to be disciples, sold-out followers of Jesus Christ, they will continue to show up, cheer, and maybe even tell their friends, but their lives may not reflect a personal, missional buy-in to the agenda of the kingdom of God and the grace of Jesus Christ. People matter too much to miss this critical distinction. God's agenda matters too much to allow this confusion.

A number of churches still count members as though the membership roll is a top-tier measurement of success. That's a membership philosophy that repels not only 20-somethings, but any kingdom-minded Christ-follower who wants more than mere association with a local club. There's a big difference between membership—even if it's growing—and forward movement. It's because of this distinction that some churches, particularly those who would consider themselves "emergent," have dropped *membership* from their practice and vocabulary.

Consider Community Christian Church in Naperville, Illinois. Dave Ferguson and his brother Jon founded this church in 1993. Along with the other members of our senior management team, I have participated in Community Christian's annual New Thing Conference. There I was able to learn firsthand about its ministry strategy through 13 distinct campuses with thousands attending their weekend gatherings. This church doesn't have any members, at least officially. No one in the church has signed a membership covenant, but thousands each year complete surveys evaluating their progress on their faith journeys and their commitment to the church. Dave and Jon just refuse to call this *membership*, just as they refuse to call Christ-followers *Christians*.

They've learned that words like *membership* and *Christian* carry enormous personal baggage that interferes with the goal of creating devoted disciples in the kingdom of God. Association with a church can become a substitute for knowing Jesus; *Christian* can become a catchphrase describing churchgoers who may not be following Jesus at all.

It's what Matt Casper (the friendly atheist) had to say about a well-intended message from Saddleback Church: "Well, where is the call to action? The challenge to make this world a better place?…The message was that you don't have to *do* anything. Just say a prayer, use the magic words, and you're in."[4]

> **W**ords like *membership* and *Christian* carry enormous personal baggage that interferes with the goal of creating devoted disciples in the kingdom of God.

Although the pastor whom Casper refers to intended to communicate the wonder of God's all-inclusive grace, Casper heard easy belief without a call to action.

Unfortunately, rather than calling people to a lifestyle that transforms not only the believer's life but also the believer's world, too many churches present Christianity and membership as mere assent to a set of beliefs. That idea is exactly what Community Christian wants to change in the minds and hearts of its people. It's why it doesn't recognize church membership.

At Granger we want people to grasp this truth: If you really believe, you'll courageously act. But we also believe that church membership can be redefined and practiced in a lifestyle consistent with the kingdom of God. We intentionally invite people to be part of the movement of God, and we intentionally invite people to express their commitment to that movement through church membership.

Given widespread misunderstandings about church membership and institutionalized religion, churches that practice membership need to accept the responsibility to deconstruct and reconstruct the true meaning of membership in the local church—that it is about joining a local community as part of a kingdom-focused movement.

> **I**f church membership (or worse yet, Christianity) is something people believe they are simply "born into," we have some serious deconstructing to do.

Free Association or Covenant?

Mark Beeson often talks with our people about the difference between free-association relationships and covenant relationships. Here's my take on his excellent teaching.

Every few years I'm invited to participate in the Stewart reunion in central Indiana. People come from the West Coast, the South, the Midwest. It can be a large gathering, but the whole country isn't invited. I'm invited because I was born into the Stewart family, my mom's side of the family. I didn't elect to be part of the family; I just am. It doesn't cost me anything to enjoy the association. I was part of it the day I was born. No choice, no cost, no commitment. In fact, I don't have to attend the reunion to be a member of the family. I am a member by free association.

There are people who look at their church relationship, even membership, in the same way. They're just born into it. Her grandfather was Baptist; so is she. His mom was Catholic; so is he. In fact, a large number of people in our country think, "I'm American; therefore, I'm a Christian." Really?

If church membership (or worse yet, Christianity) is something people believe they are simply "born into," we have some serious deconstructing to do. That kind of thinking creates a powerless organization made up of disconnected, disenchanted, disloyal "members." A similar picture could be painted of the United States, where citizenship is largely a result of birth, demanding little or no loyalty or connection.

However, a person born outside this country who meets certain requirements, including moral behavior, the ability to read and speak English, and loyalty to the Constitution, can engage in the process of becoming a U.S. citizen. This process is called naturalization, a covenant relationship that allows the individual to be accepted as a naturalized citizen. The more than 700,000 people who become citizens every year have a much different relationship with our country than those who are born here. Naturalized citizens are intentional about their "membership." It's a covenant that comes with a choice, a cost, and a commitment to belong.

How do people in your church step into that level of commitment? How do they make a definite choice to tithe, build relationships, serve, support the ministry, and share the call to live out the Great Commission and the Greatest Commandment? The choice to love, follow, and obey Christ in community comes at a significant cost.

> Church membership is not a thing of the past, even if it has been tainted by churches with no positive influence on the culture.

At Granger it is our goal to have more weekend attendees than members. That's because our ministry model is about journey. It's about steps, one at a time. We allow our guests and returning attendees time to explore the church, to listen to messages and conversations, to experience safe relationships with people who *are* members, who *are* Christ-followers. They want to know if Jesus and the claims we communicate about him are true. And we've found that they will agree or not agree over time, as they explore, listen, and experience. They want to know for themselves if the hope we keep talking about actually translates into changed lives.[5]

As they watch, listen, interact, and journey, they learn that membership is about commitment. It's a choice. There's a cost. And yes, it's worth one's time, effort, resources, talents, and energy. Nelson Searcy points out that "too many churches think it is better to continually have the same non-members in attendance than to mention membership and risk scaring them away. This backward mindset undermines the power of the Church Body as established by Christ."[6] Church membership is not a thing of the past, even if it has been tainted by churches with no positive influence on the culture. Give people time to make commitments that count, but call for commitment!

Assimilation is something else.

The Problem With Assimilation

I may be on a one-man mission to remove the word *assimilation* from church departments and job titles. I don't know that my title, pastor of connections, is the solution, but at Granger the word *assimilation* is taboo. The word alone conjures up images of cloning and coercion.

"Welcome to First Church. Come back for a second visit, and you're ours. We will assimilate you. You *will* become one of us." I really do hate the word and all its connotations.

Whether you use the word or not, the philosophy of assimilation risks creating...

- an environment in which people aren't free to explore, ask questions, and learn;

- lots of programs designed to validate the church's effectiveness in "involving" people;

- a culture of "right" beliefs, void of effectiveness but robust with clones;

- a hard-hitting sales pitch that feels coercive and sounds exclusive;

- a self-preserving, inward-focused organization;

- an agenda more focused on projects than people; and

- more connections with the institution than with people.

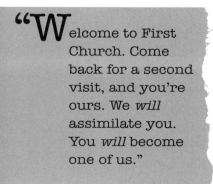

"**W**elcome to First Church. Come back for a second visit, and you're ours. We *will* assimilate you. You *will* become one of us."

Some of you will retain your "assimilation pastor" title. That's OK. Although there are risks with words and paradigms like *assimilation,* it doesn't mean they're innately bad or wrong. As I stated earlier, church membership has its own set of risks if not communicated clearly, but that doesn't mean every local church should do away with membership.

Call the process *assimilation.* Label it a *journey.* Whatever. But if you'll focus on people and the life God invites them to, you'll have your priorities straight.

From Chapter 2

Your Local Church

- If you surveyed some newer people in your church, what would they say about your expectation of their journeys? Would they say your church allows them time and space to explore and experience? Or would they say your church urges and even pressures them into belonging before they're ready? Would they say they felt respected? Here's an idea: Ask them.

- What is the *intended* approach to involving people in your church? How clear is that approach among your staff? your lead volunteers? Is everyone operating from the same plan?

- Is membership in your church associated with privilege (the right to vote, receive services from the church, an opportunity to be on the board) or with relational responsibilities (proactively supporting the mission and leadership team, leveraging talents and gifts to serve others, responding to the needs of others within personal relationships)? Is there a cost (expectations to give time, resources, and energy) associated with joining your church? If so, is that commitment clear to everyone considering membership? How can you make the cost crystal clear and elevate the commitment of belonging through membership?

Your Personal Life

- How do you respond to high-pressured tactics to make a choice you're not ready to make? How do you define *respect* when you're the one expecting it? How do you interact with people who are new or nearly new to your church? How do you intentionally convey respect for them and their personal journeys? Consider your conversations about belonging at your church; are they harsh expectations or organic invitations?

- Think about your own sense of belonging and commitment to your church. What do you suppose exploring attendees at your church would conclude about membership if they experienced *only* your personal level of commitment to relationships, serving, giving, and investing in the mission of your church?

Endnotes

1. Joseph R. Myers, *Organic Community: Creating a Place Where People Naturally Connect* (Grand Rapids, MI: Baker Books, 2007), 48.

2. Greg L. Hawkins and Cally Parkinson, with Eric Arnson, *Reveal: Where Are You?* (Barrington, IL: Willow Creek Resources, 2007), 16.

3. Rob Bell, *Velvet Elvis* (Grand Rapids, MI: Zondervan, 2005), 83.

4. Jim Henderson and Matt Casper, *Jim and Casper Go to Church: Frank Conversation about Faith, Churches, and Well-Meaning Christians* (Carol Stream, IL: Tyndale House Publishers, 2007), 6.

5. In fact, at Granger if we consider the percentage of people who are not members too small, we conclude that our Christ-following members are not living out their commitment to invest in the lives of people who do not yet know their worth before God—enough to invite them to "come and see."

6. Nelson Searcy, with Jennifer Dykes Henson, *Fusion: Turning First-Time Guests into Fully Engaged Members of Your Church* (Ventura, CA: Regal, 2007), 143-144.

You Can't Create People

> *"The real action comes next: The star in this drama, to whom I'm a mere stagehand, will change your life. I'm baptizing you here in the river, turning your old life in for a kingdom life. His baptism—a holy baptism by the Holy Spirit— will change you from the inside out."*
> —*John the Baptist*, speaking of Jesus
> (Mark 1:7, The Message)

The Burden of Responsibility *For*

I've always cared about the journeys of the people I lead. As a youth pastor, I was concerned about "my" students learning, maturing, and owning their faith. When I implemented a process by which adults could find and engage in ministry roles best suited to their wiring, I didn't rest easily until everyone had made those connections. I cared about the job performance and personal lives of my team during the few years I spent in retail management. In early 2000 when I joined Granger's staff as pastor of connections, I carried this same sense of personal responsibility for our people to connect in meaningful relationships, take courageous steps toward Christ, and develop into fully devoted followers of Jesus Christ.

I still care. I still pray. I still feel responsible. But not as I once did. And I'm really happy about that.

I still care. I still pray. I still feel responsible. But not as I once did. And I'm really happy about that.

It's not that I care less. I just don't feel responsible *for* our people. I do, however, feel responsible *to* our people.

There's a big difference.

When I felt responsible *for* every person, my failure or success depended on *their* steps in *their* journeys. When I felt responsible *for* our students, I considered their missteps to be my fault. I felt profound guilt when people didn't line up with what I thought they should know and do.

The Freedom of Responsibility *To*

Being responsible *to* our people is quite different. And incredibly freeing.

- When I'm responsible *to* people, I understand they have choices. When I'm responsible *for* people, I think I should decide for them.

- When I'm responsible *to* people, I know they must figure out their next steps. When I'm responsible *for* people, I try to tell them what their next steps are.

- When I'm responsible *to* people, I know they must bear the consequences of their own chosen actions. When I'm responsible *for* people, I assume the guilt—or worse, the shame—for them.

- When I'm responsible *to* people, I share their journeys, offering encouragement and teaching. When I'm responsible *for* people, I try to direct their journeys, never allowing them to wrestle, mess up, or make a wrong turn.

- When I'm responsible *to* people, I talk to God a lot on their behalf. When I'm responsible *for* people, I talk to people a lot on God's behalf.

A Biblical Responsibility

The Bible is clear: As a pastor I do answer to God for all that has been entrusted to me. I am to equip, shepherd, resource, and lead our people. Paul writes in Ephesians 4:11-16:

> *It was he who gave some to be apostles, some to be prophets, some to be evangelists, and some to be pastors and teachers, to prepare God's people for works of service, so that the body of Christ may be built up until we all reach unity in the faith and in the*

knowledge of the Son of God and become mature, attaining to the whole measure of the fullness of Christ.

Then we will no longer be infants, tossed back and forth by the waves, and blown here and there by every wind of teaching and by the cunning and craftiness of men in their deceitful scheming. Instead, speaking the truth in love, we will in all things grow up into him who is the Head, that is, Christ. From him the whole body, joined and held together by every supporting ligament, grows and builds itself up in love, as each part does its work.

Pastors and other church leaders have a biblical responsibility to teach and lead the local church. However, we must keep this distinction clear: Being responsible *to* people is not the same as being responsible *for* them. When we accept our responsibility *to* our people, we will experience the relief of newfound freedom. Look at this list of Scripture verses that speak to our charge:

- Ephesians 4:2: "Always be humble and gentle. Be patient with each other, making allowance for each other's faults because of your love" (New Living Translation). Paul tells us not to assume responsibility for each other's faults but, rather, to accept each other in spite of them.

- Philippians 2:4: "Don't look out only for your own interests, but take an interest in others, too" (NLT). Again, this is very different from feeling responsible for others. It requires humility, not arrogance, to be responsible *to* rather than *for*.

- 1 Thessalonians 2:4-8: "On the contrary, we speak as men approved by God to be entrusted with the gospel. We are not trying to please men but God, who tests our hearts. You know we never used flattery, nor did we put on a mask to cover up greed—God is our witness. We were not looking for praise from men, not from you or anyone else. As apostles of Christ we could have been a burden to you, but we were gentle among you, like a mother caring for her little children. We loved you so much that we were delighted to share with you not only the gospel of God but our lives as well, because you had become so dear to us." This hardly depicts a man who claimed responsibility *for* anyone; rather it's a picture of an unassuming man committed to sharing the gospel of Jesus Christ. His sense of worth in his role had nothing to do with the approval—in word or behavior—of men; his approval came from God.

- 2 Thessalonians 1:11: "Because we know that this extraordinary day is just ahead, we pray for you all the time—pray that our God will make you fit for what he's called you to be, pray that he'll fill your good ideas and acts of faith with his own energy so that it all amounts to something" (The Message). Although Paul often admonishes in his letters, he is always urging and constantly praying, understanding that it's God who has imbued his readers with eternal value, not him.

- 1 Timothy 4:11-14: "Get the word out. Teach all these things. And don't let anyone put you down because you're young. Teach believers with your life: by word, by demeanor, by love, by faith, by integrity. Stay at your post reading Scripture, giving counsel, teaching. And that special gift of ministry you were given when the leaders of the church laid hands on you and prayed—keep that dusted off and in use" (The Message). Paul conveyed to young Timothy the responsibility to teach, even to do so with authority, but Paul never indicated that Timothy was also responsible for his students' responses to his teaching.

- Matthew 28:18-20: "Then Jesus came to them and said, 'All authority in heaven and on earth has been given to me. Therefore go and make disciples of all nations, baptizing them in the name of the Father and of the Son and of the Holy Spirit, and teaching them to obey everything I have commanded you. And surely I am with you always, to the very end of the age.' " Consider The Message's rendition of this passage. I believe the tone of responsibility may be clearer in this paraphrase: "Jesus, undeterred, went right ahead and gave his charge: 'God authorized and commanded me to commission you: Go out and train everyone you meet, far and near, in this way of life, marking them by baptism in the threefold name: Father, Son, and Holy Spirit. Then instruct them in the practice of all I have commanded you. I'll be with you as you do this, day after day after day, right up to the end of the age.' "

Surely the intent of the New International Version, the New Living Translation, and The Message is not to have us shanghai people, forcing them to be disciples. Rather, we're instructed to train, to instruct, to teach.

People still get to choose how to respond.

There's Still Just One Holy Spirit

My dear wife will tell you that I spent too many years of our marriage trying to play Holy Spirit in her life. My distorted view of myself, my toxic legalism, and my perfectionism created a tyranny of expectations she could not live up to. It took me longer than I care to admit to step aside and let God be God. He wants me to love her as Christ loved the church by giving up my own agenda and dying to my own interests. The Holy Spirit will *use* me to encourage, support, and nurture her as she becomes the person God wants her to be.

Clearly we are not to be responsible *for* our spouses or our people. In their time-tested, groundbreaking book *Boundaries,* Henry Cloud and John Townsend state, "Problems arise when boundaries of responsibility are confused. We are to *love* one another, not *be* one another."[1] You can't change, create, or restore people. Only God can.

We carry unhealthy personal boundaries into relationships outside our homes and into our churches. In discussions with other church leaders and pastors, I've learned I'm not alone in this quandary. I believe we tend to misread the Scriptures *because* of our personal baggage and distortion of personal boundaries. The result is imbalanced leaders, struggling to get it right. From my observations, I believe these imbalanced leaders risk burnout, causing them to step away from church ministry. They become Bible-thumping code enforcers who browbeat their people and adopt a calloused and cynical view of people in general and often of God. We pay a high price when we misunderstand our responsibility.

Jesus was clear about the role of the Holy Spirit in our lives: "But the Counselor, the Holy Spirit, whom the Father will send in my name, will teach you all things and will remind you of everything I have said to you" (John 14:26). Jesus also says, "When he comes, he will convict the world of guilt in regard to sin and righteousness and judgment" (John 16:8). If Jesus trusts the Holy Spirit, maybe we should, too.

Paul reminds us that the Holy Spirit was not only promised to Jesus' earliest disciples but also to each of his followers today: "Do you not know that your body is a temple of the Holy Spirit, who is in you, whom you have

> **If Jesus trusts the Holy Spirit, maybe we should, too.**

received from God?" (1 Corinthians 6:19a). In 1 Thessalonians 4:7-8, Paul clearly distinguishes between our role and that of the Holy Spirit: "For God did not call us to be impure, but to live a holy life. Therefore, he who rejects this instruction does not reject man but God, who gives you his Holy Spirit."

Any questions? The office and function of the Holy Spirit are not up for grabs. He's still alive and well today.

Growth Is About Transformation

In his book *Renovation of the Heart,* Dallas Willard reminds us that our spiritual formation didn't begin when we recognized or even came to Christ, but rather our formation as spiritual beings began when we inhaled our first breath of air. Because we're created in the image of God, we're spiritual beings. There's nothing about our existence that isn't spiritual. When we think of the physical and mental as separate from the spiritual, we fail to recognize what it is to be fully human.

Willard goes on to suggest that when we commit to getting back into step with God's original purpose for our created lives, when we commit to following Jesus and his kingdom priorities, then we embark not merely on spiritual *formation* but in a new chapter of spiritual *transformation.* We begin to understand that becoming like Christ—more fully reflecting his image— involves every aspect of our existence: body, mind, soul, and spirit. To be fully human is to live an integrated life. Spiritual growth not only affects home, friendships, work, play, church, and everyday life, but also happens at home, in our friendships, through our careers, in our play, at church, and in the ups and downs of everyday life. It is a process, a journey of the heart; it is a process of transformation. [2]

Spiritual growth not only affects home, friendships, work, play, church, and everyday life, but also happens at home, in our friendships, through our careers, in our play, at church, and in the ups and downs of everyday life.

The Holy Spirit Uses People

To be human is to be spiritual. To be spiritual is to be relational. We are connected, like it or not. Cloud and Townsend put it well. God uses people to help us grow; in fact, people are God's "Plan A."[3] Being created in the image of God is the common denominator of every human being. It is the core spirituality within each of us. Our capacity for human connection is a reality, not because we are Christian, but because we are human.

Any positive change in my life I attribute to the Scriptures, to God's Spirit, to the conviction of the Holy Spirit, and to the grace of God through Jesus Christ. But do you know what else? God uses people to help me understand the Scriptures. God uses people to speak words of encouragement. God uses people to challenge my thinking and decision making. God uses people to help me hear the conviction of the Spirit and to recognize the grace of God. People are still God's Plan A. Every relationship either helps or hinders my ongoing transformation into the image of Christ.

There's not a thought in our heads, a belief in our theology, a notion in our spirits that isn't connected to another human being. What I believe today has been influenced by my parents, pastors, teachers, friends, celebrities, my wife, my daughter, small-group members, and people I don't even recognize as influencers.

It's true you can't create people. They're already created. You also can't re-create them. You can't make them grow. You can't force steps. It's not that you're somehow failing to do so; it's just not possible. It's not your job to make sure all the people in your church (or your life) are taking their next steps. They're *their* next steps, not yours. It's their responsibility, not yours. Stop trying. It's not your job. Only the Holy Spirit can transform human lives.

What Kind of Church Is Yours?

You've seen the labels. Maybe you've adopted a few.

"We're a Bible-teaching church."

"We're a seeker church."

"We're a small-groups, discipling church."

So the assumptions are that if you're a teaching church, you prioritize the Scriptures. (Of course, this generally also assumes that other churches *aren't* focused on the Scriptures.) If you're a seeker church, you center everything

> **T**his infighting makes me tired. We're created by the same God. We're following the same Jesus. We're empowered by the same Spirit. We are God's church, reflecting the image of Jesus Christ to our culture.

in your ministry on those who aren't following Jesus but are searching for God in some way. (Of course, the Bible-teaching church might assume that the seeker church isn't teaching the entire Word of God and is concerned only with "saving" people, not helping them know God through a biblical understanding of him.) If you're a discipling church, you do something that both the teaching church and the seeker church fail to do. You make disciples in small groups as commanded by Jesus in Matthew 28 and modeled by the early church in Acts 2 and 4.

This infighting makes me tired. We're created by the same God. We're following the same Jesus. We're empowered by the same Spirit. We are God's church, reflecting the image of Jesus Christ to our culture. Maybe some seeker churches are teaching the Bible *and* making disciples. Maybe some teaching churches are reaching seekers *and* watching disciples grow. Maybe some discipling churches are teaching the Scriptures *and* seeing seekers come to faith in Jesus Christ. In fact, there's no "maybe" about it. Churches all over the globe are reaching seekers, teaching the truth of the Scriptures, and discipling people in the context of healthy relationships.

What Do We Expect?

Have you ever watched a couple move from marital bliss to living hell? Perhaps you know a couple whose point of contention centered around sexuality. Or finances. Or communication. Most of the time the cause of the conflict starts well outside the bedroom, before the first dollar is spent, prior to the first conversation or argument. It begins with misaligned expectations. She expects one thing; he expects another. Unfortunately, when reality doesn't match our expectations, only one thing fills the space between the two: disappointment.

This happens in churches all the time.

People expect their churches to be solely responsible for their growth. People expect their churches to feed them. People expect their churches to find them a friend. People expect their churches to use the right language, support the right causes, interpret the Scriptures the right way, and go about spiritual transformation in the right way. But for most Christians the "right" way is generally "their" way.

People expect if the church is teaching the Bible, seeing people come to Christ, and making disciples, the church will be filled with "mature" Christians. Mark Beeson posted these thoughts on his blog (MarkBeeson.com), along with a picture of a wild male turkey in his backyard.

It's Easter weekend and we're in the middle of a blizzard!

What do I see when I look out my window? This male turkey scratching in the snow and leaves. His beard indicates he's mature. In a few weeks he'll breed as many hens as possible and we'll end up with little turkey poults running all over the place.

If you have mature birds you'll soon have immature *birds; that's the way it works.*

Three days ago Rick Warren proffered this question for me to mull over: What is the mature church?

I knew immediately how I would respond.

The "mature church" is the church filled with immaturity.

Anywhere in the world, whether plant or animal, the clear delineation of maturity *is the ability to reproduce. Immature animals can't reproduce. Immature plants can't replicate themselves. The definition of maturity is* "being fully ripe, fully aged" *so the connotation of maturity is obvious. Where you see maturity you'll observe new life, babies and immaturity all over the place.*

Maturity desires reproduction.

Maturity tolerates juvenile behavior (from juveniles) while training its progeny for success in life.

Maturity means "little poults running all over the place."

If you attend a mature church, be prepared for immaturity.

Where you find mature Christians you'll find little "babes in Christ" *running all over the place. In fact, if you have been looking for a church where* "everyone tithes" *or* "everyone serves" *you are not looking for a mature church, you are looking for a dying church—aged, impotent and bereft of spiritual newborns—because* "everyone" *is mature.*

Few things are more disturbing than a flock of adult believers standing around complaining that "no one has come to Christ" *while refusing to do something that might result in new life.*

So when you bump into someone who acts "immature" *at one of our Easter services, don't complain, and don't be surprised. Instead, thank God the* "mature in Christ" *are busy delivering newborn babies to the family of God.*[4]

Whose Expectations?

I contend that the disappointment Christians feel within their local churches is almost always a matter of false expectations. Of course, those expectations exist on both sides of the aisle. In *Reveal*, the 2007 survey conducted by Willow Creek Community Church, some of these false expectations were exposed. In discussing this study, Bill Hybels stated that the goal of the church is to help believers become independent. He went on to say that the local church should prioritize the work of introducing people to Jesus and then help them develop to a certain point on their journey. After that they should feed themselves and join the church in bringing more people to Jesus Christ.[5]

The church at large has expected that people should own their journeys with Christ. They should be practicing spiritual disciplines that develop their intimacy with God and poise them for growth in their experiences, relationships, service, and exploration of the Scriptures. They should

be helping others on the journey. They
should be caring for the world God longs
to restore. They should be investing in
relationships with people.

At the same time, Christians have commonly
expected the local church to teach everything
that can be learned about the Bible. They've expected the church to
formally organize every friendship circle for relational growth. They've
expected the church to identify the community's needs and allocate time,
money, and energy accordingly.

In short, the church's expectations haven't been aligned with those of the
people. And that leaves pastors *and* people disappointed.

Of course there's one other possible cause for disappointment: *false*
expectations. What if church leaders have expected the same thing the
people have expected—that the church *is* responsible for people's spiritual
growth and that the church *should be* the provider of every class, resource,
and group to further that growth? What if *both* the pastor *and* the people
have shared these expectations?

There will still be grave disappointment because it's not how we're designed
to function. The church is not merely an institution; it's a group of people
in relationship with one another. The church is not a program; it's a living
organism. The church is not a servant to man; it's a collection of people
who are serving God and man.

What If We Raised the Expectation?

In his book *Called: Becoming Who You Were Born to Be,* Kary Oberbrunner
lays out a fundamental contrast between what we in the church often expect
and what we should expect. He observes that a common understanding
of discipleship includes this trajectory:

1. Accept Jesus and ask him into your heart.

2. Don't do bad things now.

3. Withdraw from culture.

4. Hang out with Christians.

> In short, the church's
> expectations haven't
> been aligned with
> those of the people.

5. Go to church.

6. Read your Bible and pray.

7. Be happy that you are saved and not going to hell.

8. Tell other people about how happy they can be if they follow those seven steps.

He challenges that depiction of a passionless life, suggesting that Jesus actually calls us in this way:

1. I want your whole life—everything—including your heart, soul, mind, and strength.

2. I want to form myself in you.

3. I want to transform you and then have you transform culture.

4. I want you to be in the world as I was.

5. I want you to be the church, the incarnation of me.

6. I want you to embody the Word to others.

7. I am giving you abundant life now and will do so throughout eternity.

8. Be my hands and feet in this world and see people as people, not projects to convert.[6]

> We're still committed to teaching the Scriptures as the means to revealing God's story and the invitation Christ makes to every seeker to join him in his kingdom agenda. In short, we're committed to making disciples.

At Granger we're not altering our intention to be a church who loves spiritual seekers. We believe every man, woman, boy, and girl matters to God. We won't back away from our radical commitment to leverage the culture to win the people who live in the culture. Because of that we're also still committed to teaching the Scriptures as the means to revealing God's story and the invitation Christ makes to every seeker to join him in his kingdom agenda. In short, we're committed to making disciples.

What if all the Christ-followers in your church understood that following Jesus is about

- creating a new heaven and a new earth (in every way: economically, socially, environmentally, politically, and spiritually)?

- remembering the profound life-change they celebrated years ago? (Namely, that life is not about them; it's about their pursuit of God and their love for others who matter to him.)

- their personal responsibility to not only feed themselves but to also help younger and fellow Christ-followers grow in their love of God and others?

10 Questions

I encourage you to ask these questions about the spiritual-transformation process in your church:

1. How is spiritual transformation defined in our church?
2. What do we expect of our people?
3. What do our people expect of the church?
4. How will we align our expectations of spiritual growth with those of the people?
5. In what ways is spiritual transformation expressed in our mission, vision, and values?
6. How are we trusting or not trusting the Holy Spirit to transform the lives of our people?
7. Does the spiritual-transformation process feel like an "add-on" to everything else we're doing, or is it integrated into the fabric of our church life?
8. Is there evidence that our people are engaging in spiritual transformation as a part of their lifestyles? If not, what's preventing them?
9. What key words, what specific vocabulary, and what important concepts will we use to cast vision and create a culture of spiritual transformation that is embraced by our people?
10. How do we help our people engage in spiritual disciplines as pathways rather than tasks to mark off their to-do lists?

However You Define It, Define It Simply

However you sort, align, and state expectations for spiritual transformation, I urge you to keep it simple.

However you sort, align, and state expectations for spiritual transformation, I urge you to keep it simple. At Granger we've maintained our focus from the day the church was started in 1986: "Helping people take their next step toward Christ…together."

This means that we will be a people who are committed to the Greatest Commandment and the Great Commission. We will continually take steps that identify us as people who love God and love others. Because we love God and the people who matter to him, we will actively reach out to seekers, teaching them to follow Christ in full devotion, living up to his character and conduct to bring "up there" down here.

It's that simple for us.

How simple is it for you?

After working to answer the question "What does the mature believer, transformed into the image of Christ, look like?" the pastoral team at Heights Church in Prescott, Arizona, arrived at the following definition of the "end product":

1. Mature believers have a realistic view of self, of others, and of the world.

2. Mature believers live in the "here and now" while maintaining a kingdom focus.

3. Mature believers display an ever-increasing presence of the marks of discipleship.[7]

I don't believe there is one right method for the local church to employ to help our people develop into fully devoted followers of Jesus Christ. I do not believe there is one answer for the way you encourage relationships within your church. I do not believe there is one answer for the way you address the relational spaces within your church. I do not believe you are responsible *for* your people.

So if we're not responsible for our people, what are we responsible for? Keep reading.

From Chapter 3

Your Local Church

■ Does your church demonstrate responsibility *for* or *to* the people and their spiritual growth? In what ways are you responsible for or to them? In what ways has this issue created tension in your church? Are leaders or pastors resented? Are people devalued in any way? How can your church reach agreement regarding these expectations?

■ In what ways is it apparent that your church trusts and expects the Holy Spirit to work in people's lives?

■ Work through the "10 Questions" exercise (p. 47), but do so appropriately: with others—your fellow board members, your staff team, your ministry team. Do so in a constructive, conversational manner, void of blame and full of grace.

■ What if maturity were defined in the context of the Greatest Commandment and the Great Commission? How would that definition alter commonly held expectations of discipleship in your church? Based on these two benchmark passages, make a list of no more than seven characteristics that paint a picture of a fully devoted follower of Jesus.

Your Personal Life

■ Do others see you as responsible *for* them or *to* them? Get personal: Include your spouse (if you're married), your children, other family members, and your friends. Are you controlling, worrisome, manipulative, impatient, or easily angered when it comes to your expectations of these people? If so, you—or they—could be confusing your responsibility *to* with your responsibility *for*. Pick up the book *Boundaries*. Get it today!

■ Where do you see the Holy Spirit working in your life? What has God done in you in the past 10 years? in the past five years? in the past six months? What or whom has he used to work in your life?

■ In what ways could you take more responsibility for your own spiritual journey? Consider spiritual disciplines, community, personal reading, and study. What step will you take in the next 24 hours to enhance your own experience with God?

Endnotes

1. Henry Cloud and John Townsend, *Boundaries: When to Say Yes, When to Say No to Take Control of Your Life* (Grand Rapids, MI: Zondervan, 1992), 86.

2. Dallas Willard, *Renovation of the Heart: Putting on the Character of Christ* (Colorado Springs, CO: NavPress, 2002), 19-23.

3. Henry Cloud and John Townsend, *How People Grow: What the Bible Reveals About Personal Growth* (Grand Rapids, MI: Zondervan, 2001), 120.

4. Mark Beeson at markbeeson.com/mark_beeson/2008/03/it-is-easter-we.html. Used by permission.

5. Tim Stevens at leadingsmart.com/leadingsmart/2007/02/qa_with_bill_hy.html. Used by permission.

6. Kary Oberbrunner, *Called: Becoming Who You Were Born to Be* (Winona Lake, IN: BMH Books), 8. Used by permission of the author. karyoberbrunner.com.

7. Mark Waltz at becausepeoplematter.com/marks_weblog/2007/02/spiritual_trans .html#comments.

Starbucks, Stories, and Space

"We are the third place in the lives of millions of our customers. We are the coffee that brings people together every day around the world to foster conversation and community."
—Howard Schultz[1]

Starbucks Gets It

In 2008, Howard Schultz returned to the Starbucks Corporation as CEO to re-establish the company's commitment to being America's "third place."[2]

Schultz wasn't the first to coin the phrase *third place*. The term was introduced by Ray Oldenburg, who defines it as "a generic designation for a great variety of public places that host the regular, voluntary, informal, and happily anticipated gatherings of individuals beyond the realms of home and work."[3]

If there are, indeed, three primary places in our lives—work, home, and community—then our churches certainly could occupy that third place, a place where people feel at home.[4]

I believe the local church needs to carefully create this kind of third place not only for our newest guests but for all our guests, returning friends, and members. The church can do this by creating lasting impressions. If first impressions are about connection, lasting impressions are about relationships.

If first impressions are about connection, lasting impressions are about relationships.

Regarding third places, Oldenburg continues, "Conversation is the primary activity and the major vehicle for the display and appreciation of human personality and individuality."[5]

Oldenburg didn't write this with the church in mind. Rather, he was thinking of places like bars, salons, and coffee shops. We can't ignore the fact that business has learned more about people's innate needs and desires than the church has. The local church must pay attention not only to the human desire for connection but also to the strategic approach we take to create places and spaces for such interaction. People want a third place, not just to drink a good cup of coffee but also to nurture relationships. What better place to fulfill this need than in the local church?

A Tale of Two Trips

I've been to India twice. On both occasions I took a trip to Agra to visit the Red Fort and the famed Taj Mahal.

During my first tour, I was accompanied by a native travel guide who immersed herself in the history and legacy of her country. She told stories about the people and events as though she had experienced them herself. She was connected with the story and told it as if it were her own. I listened with keen interest. I was invited into her world, her history, her life. I not only felt I knew her country and her heritage; I believed I knew *her*.

On the second tour, I was traveling with my family and was eager for them to experience all I had in my first Eastern adventure. As we embarked on the two-hour ride from New Delhi to Agra, my excitement waned as our escort behaved more like a hired Atlas map than a tour guide. He got us to our destination, pointing to all the important sites along the way. He knew the land and its history, but he wasn't personally involved. There was no connection, no fun.

The first guide had invited me on a journey filled with surprise and wonder. The second merely spoke above the noise of the taxi. As a result, my first trip was personal and relational; the second was impersonal and rigid.

I fear that in many churches the approach to helping people take steps in their journeys toward and with God has more nearly paralleled my second Agra excursion: dry, unenthusiastic, void of relationship or enjoyment.

Mark Beeson has often observed, "It has taken the church 2,000 years to make Jesus Christ—the most winsome person who ever lived—boring!" Jesus was a revolutionary leader who announced that the kingdom of God had come to earth in the here and now. When the local church reduces discipleship to a regimented curriculum, we turn the adventure of following Jesus into a dreary list of activities to check off, a dusty, boring tour of lifeless information.

At Granger we intentionally create environments—weekend services, Bible classes, retreats, small groups gatherings, serving events, and volunteer teams—that allow people to join others on the journey. Bible teaching provides a critical foundation for theology, and relationships provide a critical context for that teaching to be processed. Real-life stories are exchanged. Real-life change is experienced. Serving introduces people to lives beyond themselves. They see and hear stories that break down socioeconomic, racial, and geographical barriers. In these stories people see themselves, and they are confronted with the all-embracing grace of God.

As we share our lives and our stories unfold in the context of our relationships, we become invested in the journey—our own and those of the people next to us. We not only hear God's story; we also experience it with one another.

Disciples' lives are changed by the power of a winsome Christ. Disciples live life to the max (John 10:10) as they love God and others more and more. Disciples grow up to lean into the lives of other disciples around them, listening carefully to their stories, sharing the story of their own journeys and the story of God. It's rich, full of mystery, discovery, and transformation. It's the story of God's interaction with those he created in his own image.

And that really is the point: Individuals' stories of life transformation intersect with the stories of others who need to hear how much they matter to Christ.

> When the local church reduces discipleship to a regimented curriculum, we turn the adventure of following Jesus into a dreary list of activities to check off, a dusty, boring tour of lifeless information.

Space for Relationships

In his book *The Search to Belong: Rethinking Intimacy, Community, and Small Groups,* Joseph Myers cites a study conducted in the 1960s by sociologist Edward T. Hall. Hall's work was about physical space and how it influences culture and communication (proxemics). He identified four spaces of human interaction: public, social, personal, and intimate.[6] Myers explores these four spaces within the framework of community. I won't attempt to relate his full hypothesis here (you'll have to buy his book), but I will try to summarize and apply it.

Public space exists in your weekend service. Whether your crowd is large or small, if your church is growing at all, not everyone knows everyone else. However, people gather around a common purpose. In most cases people who show up for a weekend church service are there for hope and help of some kind. They share enough in common that following a service they could share a friendly exchange about the message or the music. They don't have to be friends to share in this kind of exchange. It's public space.

The second space of human interaction is social space. This space can exist in a variety of sizes of crowds or groups. A defining characteristic is small talk—light but connective conversation about common life experiences. Pointing to people's innate need for social interaction, Myers states, "Take away social relationships and our *community conversation* becomes flat, lacking a spontaneous connection to the entirety of our relationships."[7] Not only is lighthearted conversation typical in social space, it's necessary. Our ability to enter into transformative relationships is actually dependent on lighter conversation. The small talk may range from the weather to shared family experiences to a universal and specific topic at hand.

For example, let's say a service focuses on finances and stewardship. In that public space, it's highly unlikely that someone will stand and announce to everyone, "You nailed me between the eyes, Pastor! I'm a mess; my finances are a mess. I need help." Nope, not very likely.

However, during that service, let's say several dozen people decide to participate in a four-week workshop to explore their finances and get help with their budgets. In that setting, social space is created. Not everyone from the weekend service participates. It's a smaller venue with a narrow focus: help with money. Naturally, the conversation is more specific than in the public space of the weekend service. Merely by their attendance, every person in the workshop conveys to everyone else, "I could benefit from this experience."

It's likely that during the course of their four weeks together, a man or woman may connect well with a few other people. Bob, Trevor, and Gary may spend several hours over the month getting better acquainted. They aren't tight buds, but they discover that they work in the same industry and live in the same area of the city. At the final workshop, they decide to connect over coffee on Tuesday mornings before they go to the office. The conversation becomes even more focused: Bob tells Trevor and Gary that his financial decisions have cost him his marriage. Trevor asks for help in finding an investment planner because he's not considered how he'll provide for his family past retirement. The conversation has turned personal because an appropriate amount of trust has been established over time. The space has moved from social to personal.

The final space—intimacy—is entered, not by all three of these men, but by two of them. Again, as trust is tested and deepened over time, Bob and Trevor build a friendship that surprises both of them. Bob is surprised and relieved one morning when he hears himself saying to Trevor, "I didn't just lose my first marriage over money matters; I'm about to lose my current marriage. My wife told me she wants a divorce. She discovered my 20-year gambling addiction that's draining our bank account. I'm in over my head with debt and addiction. I need help."

That level of relationship, says Myers, is slow to develop and hard to find. He suggests that most of us will have only five to six intimate relationships in our lifetimes—and up to half of those will be with relatives.

Ultimately, every society acknowledges this innate desire for relationships. Relationship defines us. It is the *Imago Dei*, the image of God, stamped on our lives. Before people ever experience personal or intimate space, they need social and public space where they believe they fit, where they can feel comfortable enough to be who they are, to be real. People need a third place.

> Relationship defines us. It is the *Imago Dei*, the image of God, stamped on our lives.

Your Corporate Story Matters

Think about your own family. What kinds of stories are told every year around the Christmas tree or over a Thanksgiving turkey? They are the same kinds of stories that are told in my living room and at my mom's kitchen table. Stories about the past. And they're always the same stories.

- That accident in the family station wagon when my head got lodged between the seat and the car wall and my eyes rolled back in my head, so my mom thought I was dead. (Really, it happened. And it's always told the same way.)

- The story about my brother's arm bleeding and some connection with my pocket knife. (I always get confused about how that story goes.)

- Or the story about Grandpa shooting himself in the shoulder as he crossed a fence during a hunting expedition.

The stories of days gone by are powerful. They remind us of our roots. They help us form our identities. They anchor us. They remind us we're not alone. We need these stories.

The people in your church need these stories. How the church started. Its original vision. The first building. The fire of '72. The new building. The numbers of baptisms over the years. The work that's been accomplished on foreign soil because of the generous giving in the past. These are anchor points. They form identity. They celebrate family and a sense of belonging.

Remember, not everyone was there in the early years. Your newest guest knows nothing of the fire of '72. But the story needs to be told. Belonging is partly about embracing roots, heritage, beginnings.

There's a second aspect of the corporate story that must be shared, and that's the future. What's the vision for tomorrow?

Many extended families no longer share a vision for the future. There are no plans for trips together, few conversations about common goals. There may be a scheduled date to share a meal together, so everyone can do… what? Talk about the past. If that's all your church talks about, it won't be enough to help your guests move from visiting to belonging.

But if a compelling vision is cast, if everyone is invited to be part of what's coming, if new and old alike are needed to make the vision a reality, then the impulse to belong will be greater. So dream, envision, get a picture of what God wants to do through and in your church, and tell stories of what is yet to be. People want to belong to a story that is still being written.

> **P**eople want to belong to a story that is still being written.

Get Physical

To make the church a true third place, it must be a public place that hosts "the regular, voluntary, informal, and happily anticipated gatherings of individuals"; we must design physical spaces that encourage people to linger. Churches that are intentional about this are building coffee bars, cafés, nests of soft seating in their lobbies—not to be hip and cool, but to say, "Stay awhile…We believe relationships matter, so use this space for conversation—with God and with one another."

- At North Point Community Church in Alpharetta, Georgia, an entire hallway is lined with individual "living rooms" for this purpose.

- Heartland Community Church in Rockford, Illinois, has lined its spacious hallways with couches, encouraging impromptu conversations in a space that in most churches is designed to "keep people moving."

- The long-range plan at River Pointe Church outside of Houston, Texas, will take advantage of their typical warm, sunny days (something we take pictures of in northern Indiana). Their ultimate design will create a "city walk"—open courtyard space among several separate buildings, providing outdoor and indoor seating areas to maximize the invitation to community. The entire campus is being designed for the community to utilize throughout the week, including a stocked fishing pond, kids' play areas, sport fields and courts, bookstore, and café.

- At Granger we've expanded our atrium to include a seven-day per week restaurant where guests can share a meal or a cup of coffee. During service times they can take in the experience via multiple flat screens located throughout the space.

- Throughout the spacious lobby of Northland: A Church Distributed (Orlando, Florida), couches, loveseats, and oversized chairs invite guests to gather and visit.

Churches around the globe are recognizing the value of this third place. In doing so we are not suggesting that our people should leave Starbucks and become cloistered in the church building. There are plenty of people we can engage in a community coffee shop that just aren't ready for a visit to church. However, when churches intentionally create this kind of space, we communicate that church is a safe place. Real conversations about real-life experiences can take place with real people in a comfortable, homelike setting. God's not in a church café more than he is in a Starbucks. But I know people at Granger who sit in our café every weekend to experience the service because they feel safe there. It's their starting place, their you-are-here "x."

> Conversation cultivates the opportunity for rapport and perhaps even relationship.

Connection for a guest at your church may initially occur around a resonating topic or physical space, but ultimately that space invites storytelling conversation. And conversation cultivates the opportunity for rapport and perhaps even relationship.

Do Our Churches Get It?

Myers points to churches' tendency to undervalue these relational spaces, particularly public and social. In our teaching, vision-casting, and prayer, we concentrate on the last two spaces: personal and intimate. We have a propensity to try to move people as quickly as possible to personal and intimate relationships, as though the first two spaces are somehow shallow and meaningless. However, when we disregard the way God has designed us, when we ignore the protective walls people erect around themselves, we miss opportunities to help them make legitimate and life-altering connections.

Four Spaces of Relational Interaction

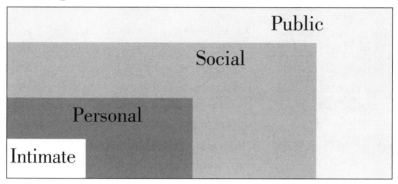

Consider your own church experience. Then visit a couple of churches in your area in the next month. Review their programs. Notice what's traditionally highlighted.

- Sunday School—Often a smaller group of people led by a teacher who uses a lecture format (either live or DVD-based). "Students" face the lectern, with little to no interaction among themselves, meeting in a sterile, white room in the church building. It's an academic setting that looks like it might be social space, except the study often fills the entire time period, leaving little to no occasion for small talk.

- Small Groups—Again, a smaller group of people, this time meeting in homes. The invitation often requires a jump from the weekend service (public space) to the private home of a stranger, with the encouragement to "get real" in "real relationships" (suggesting personal or intimate space).

- Men's Ministry—Although some promote a breakfast setting (suggesting social space), too many use language such as "accountability" and the classic Proverbs-based "iron sharpens iron" relationship (personal or intimate space).

- Women's Ministry—Women seem to do better at this than men, often offering niche-interest gatherings. However, promotions for women's ministry often suggest the event or group will allow women to "go deeper" in their relationships (personal or intimate space).

- Prayer Meetings—These gatherings are almost immediately perceived as events for the "mature" Christ-follower, where every wall comes down as people seek God together (personal or intimate space).

The list could go on and on. Go ahead; add your own observations.

Are these offerings wrong? Not necessarily. In fact, many of us can recall life-changing experiences stemming from one or more of these settings. But usually these opportunities don't serve as effective means to connect newer guests, especially the unchurched, because the movement from public space (the weekend service) to one of these other venues (personal or intimate space) is not a step—it's a quantum leap. And most people will not make the jump.

So whether you cancel meetings or eliminate ministries (yes, we did... read Chapter 6), pay attention to basic human behavior and the innate need for relationships that are public and social in nature. Help people take steps that are doable as well as attractive rather than improbable and scary (more on this in Chapter 7).

I Didn't Get It

I grew up in the church. Not Granger Community Church, but I've been in a church since I was 2 weeks old. Granted I don't remember those early weeks and years, but I'm told I was a regular attendee from the get-go. In fact, the closest I've ever come to being like Jesus was when I was left at the church building one Sunday night. Doors were locked. Lights were out. I was alone. No scribes, no teachers, no pastors being enlightened by my questions and insightful observations of the Torah. That's where the similarities between Jesus and me end. But I did grow up in the church.

I had God-loving pastors and Jesus-following leaders, but my sense of community was rather underdeveloped. Most of my early church experiences seemed to focus on getting *it* right. And *it*—a performance-based list of do's and don'ts—was everything. I don't know if people were aware they were writing such prescriptive expectations, and I don't know if anyone stopped to evaluate the dysfunction of the pharisaical religion they embraced.

In any case, my understanding of relationships was limited to two primary teachings:

- "You don't need relationships with sinners (people not following Jesus). Their godless, evil influence will drag you down. Have nothing to do with them. Cut them off. Flee."

- "You need Christians around you to hold you accountable, to help you monitor your performance as a Christian. They'll help you do what you need to do and help you see when you're doing something wrong."

So I grew up believing that sharing my story in relationships with other Christians would be personal, if not intimate. Relationships experienced in public or social space would never be enough. The role of other Christians was to help me perform better, get *it* right. Like a bad-tasting medicine, the relationship might not always feel good, but it would be for my own good. That's what I was told anyway.

The role of other Christians was to help me perform better, get *it* right. Like a bad-tasting medicine, the relationship might not always feel good, but it would be for my own good. That's what I was told anyway.

On the contrary, I *didn't* grow up understanding that everyone I passed in the school hallway, saw in band, sat next to in science class, and rode with on the school bus had intrinsic value to God. I didn't understand that their stories mattered. No one had told me, "You'll never look into the eyes of another human being who does not matter to God." In fact, I assumed that if they didn't attend church and experience God as I did, then they were the enemy. They were dangerous to my pursuit of God. The only valuable exchange I could have with them would be my "testimony," my "witness." And that certainly wasn't about relationship; it was about "rescuing the perishing." Good and evil. Right and wrong. And I knew where I stood. Except on those days when I knew I didn't measure up because I wasn't good enough. But I was trying, and that was more than could be said for my obviously self-centered classmates.

It embarrasses me to write this. I viewed my peers with scathing judgment. I thought my posture and verdict made me a little more like Jesus. I couldn't have been more wrong.

I'm Starting to Get It

Over the past 30 years, I've been in a lot of churches. I've been an attendee, a volunteer, a volunteer leader, and a staff pastor. I've also worked in the marketplace as a coach, salesman, job counselor, and manager. I've lived in the Midwest and the Northwest. I've had friends in the church who've loved Jesus and friends outside of the church who didn't understand at all that Jesus loved them. I've had friends who've come and gone and many who've come and never gone. And I've gained the friendship of a lifetime with my high school sweetheart, my wife.

Throughout all these experiences, places, and relationships, I've taught and been taught. I've studied and been studied. I've counseled and been counseled. I've told my story and listened to stories. I still have memories of ecstatic, mountaintop highs and wish-I-could-forget-them-forever lows.

As I consider some of my most meaningful relationships, I recognize a common factor. They all began with casual hang time, time that allowed us just to get acquainted. There was no agenda. No planning. No teaching. Just being. And in that space I recognized their innate value and discovered that even my friends who weren't Christians valued me.

That was social space. Just social space.

I needed that space before I could really understand and embrace personal and intimate relationships.

In fact, over time with four or five of those friends, the relationships were safe enough for me to choose to be completely real, to fully unpack my story. Not out of obligation, but out of my need and desire. Not because my destiny depended on it, but because my soul did. Not because I was pressured, but because I was invited. I learned these friends were not merely interested in holding me accountable, but they were genuinely curious about me, whatever that curiosity revealed.

Although I was raised in the church and have served as a pastor in more than a couple, it has been through these personal and intimate relationships that I've come to understand God's relentless grace. It *is* amazing. People bear his image. If we pay attention to what God is up to, we'll understand that there is an organic journey that is not dependent upon our programming, classes, or groups, but solely on the reality of the Holy Spirit showing up in relationships, drawing soul to soul. His work in human relationships is absolutely life changing: in intimate, personal, social, and even public spaces.

From Chapter 4

Your Local Church

- What physical environments in your church reflect a third place, inviting people to converse and interact? What capacity do you have to create or enhance this space?

- Evaluate each of your environments—weekend services, midweek services, groups, events, retreats, affinity ministries, Sunday school classes—and determine the respective space (public, social, personal) each represents. Are you pleased with the opportunities available to people to connect and relate to others? Which environments do you need to tweak? eliminate? re-create?

- In what ways does your vision invite newer people to belong, to be part of what God is doing in your church?

Your Personal Life

- What's your third place—your home away from home? *Who* makes that place feel like home to you?

- Make a list of the people with whom you currently share personal or intimate space. Recall the public and social spaces you shared before moving into deeper relationships. What were the circumstances or conversations that enabled you to move into personal or intimate space?

- Name at least three things you can do to make your church a third place, where conversation is encouraged and people feel at home.

Endnotes

1. Howard Schultz Transformation Agenda Communication #8, February 25, 2008, starbucks.com/aboutus/pressdesc.asp?id=833.

2. Starbucks chairman Schultz returning as CEO, msnbc.msn.com/id/22544023.

3. Ray Oldenburg, *The Great Good Place: Cafés, Coffee Shops, Bookstores, Bars, Hair Salons, and Other Hangouts at the Heart of a Community* (New York: Marlowe & Company, 1999), 16.

4. Ibid., 22.

5. Ibid., 42.

6. Joseph R. Myers, *The Search to Belong: Rethinking Intimacy, Community, and Small Groups*, (El Cajon, CA: Zondervan/Youth Specialties, 2003), 36.

7. Ibid., 46.

Be an Environmental Architect

"You can't just look for interesting design devices. You have to discover the heart and soul of a project. Only then will you have a fighting chance of bringing the space to life."
—*David Rockwell,* architect[1]

Now What?

In 1997, I stepped away from full-time staff ministry for a season to attend to some family relationships that had gotten rather messy as I was growing up. After living in the great Northwest for half a dozen years, my wife, daughter, and I moved across the country so I could assume a new job in retail sales. Basically, that meant I worked at the mall. A lot. I managed a men's clothing store, working 70-plus hours each week to develop a team and set a positive sales trajectory.

While I was working at the mall, our family discovered Granger Community Church. After attending services for a few months, I watched scores of people decide to follow Jesus during one Sunday morning service. Tears filled my eyes as I watched person after person acknowledge God's gift of grace. The tears really started to fall as I wondered, "What now? How do they grow now? How do they know what to do?"

These were legitimate questions, and they still are. But in that moment, I was thinking someone should be responsible *for* them. The weight seemed crushing, and I felt powerless. Within three years of that experience, I became a part of Granger's full-time staff as pastor of connections. And by that time I had come to appreciate the culture I was about to protect and help lead.

DNA Matters

The simplicity of our mission statement is affirming to guests when they first visit our church: *Helping people take their next step toward Christ… together.* Guests have taken a first step just by showing up. That step may have been one of the most difficult ones they have ever taken in their lives. That's worth affirming.

There's always a next step. For everyone. Always. The point is to take that step toward Christ intentionally. And we do so together. No lone wolves. No islands. And we *help*, but we don't take the next step *for* anyone.

All of this is part of our DNA.

By the time I stepped into my new role, I knew who we were. Three years into my Granger experience, I had watched hundreds and hundreds of people make new commitments to follow Jesus. And every time I cried. But now I don't cry because I feel responsible for them. I cry out of sheer joy. I'm thrilled to observe these people take this culminating step after taking hundreds of tiny steps. I know that our DNA of next steps will continue to be critical in their journeys. But now after 12 years as their pastor, I also know I'm not responsible *for* them.

Space for Stories

Well before people commit to following Jesus at Granger or at your church, they're taking steps. Their formation as spiritual beings has been underway all their lives. We have no idea what the Holy Spirit has been doing in their story lines before they show up in our churches. Tim Keel notes, "Throughout history people have told stories and been shaped by them, and in doing so they have discovered and constructed ways of understanding who they are and what is happening in the world around them."[2]

So it's critical that we give people space to explore, understand, and tell their stories. I'm not responsible *for* anyone's story. But I have accepted the responsibility for creating and enhancing spaces where people can take their next steps in the context of those stories.

Think Like a Designer

Straight up—I'm asking church leaders and pastors to stop feeling responsible for *people* and begin to take responsibility for *environments.* Become an environmental architect. Each setting where people in your church gather is an environment: your weekend service, your Sunday school, your groups, your retreats, your grand events.

Yves Behar is a leading innovator in design. He has worked with the likes of Coca-Cola, Johnson & Johnson, Kodak, and MIT. He thinks function and then combines emotional and aesthetic factors to create something unique.

As I read Behar's axioms, I can't help thinking of the responsibility I have accepted in helping to create relational environments at Granger. Environments that define and expand our culture and mission. Environments for staff, leaders, members, attendees, and new guests.

The following is my take on Behar's axioms[3] as they apply to the local church. I encourage you to keep them in mind as you design and build environments to effectively involve your people.

- The way you develop environments reflects your respect and caring for people. If you treat people well from a spiritual, environmental, emotional, and aesthetic standpoint, your environment's design will reflect that.

- The development of relational environments is not a short-term solution to a present problem. It must become a planning paradigm over the long haul that affects everything connected to your members and guests. This includes how the gospel connects to the weekend series and how the weekend series connects to promotion and how promotion connects to a family and how the family connects to next steps.

- You won't always get it right. You must be able to quickly adjust variables such as physical settings, start times, programming, and content. A failed approach isn't a sign of failure; it's an indication of fluidity and innovation.

- The development of relational environments must be led by senior-level leadership. Pastors, elders, and church boards need to be in touch with and embrace the innovative and creative endeavors of the church.

- Your church's approach to creating space for human interaction will not look like every other church's. Mimicking someone else's design isn't the solution. Your community, church, and mission are unique; develop your environments accordingly.

Mimicking someone else's design isn't the solution.

In their comparison of simple churches with complex churches, Thom Rainer and Eric Geiger note, "Simple church leaders are designers. They design opportunities for spiritual growth. Complex church leaders are programmers. They run ministry programs."[4] I'm inviting you to design, not program.

Plan Like an Architect

Before drawing schematics, an architect asks a number of questions of the homeowner or commercial developer. The answers to these questions reveal the function of the space, which in turn determines its design.

A similar approach is necessary in understanding, designing, and developing human environments within the local church. If you were to own the architectural responsibility for every environment in your church, what kinds of questions might you ask? Add more to this list if you'd like, but be sure to address the following five questions.

- **What's the purpose of this environment?**

An architect will ask, "Is this a residence? a business? Will it be used seasonally? year round? Is it a retreat or a daily dwelling? What is its purpose?"

The overarching purpose of any environment in the local church is to be a place where people can see Jesus Christ and take steps toward and with him. Hang on to that. Now narrow the focus a bit more. Get specific about each setting.

For instance, what's the purpose of your small groups?

- growth through shared experiences?
- increased knowledge?
- friendship?
- cook-offs?

Develop group settings to fulfill a specific purpose. If you fail to identify the purpose of each environment, people will have varying expectations of it. Remember, when experiences don't meet expectations, people are disappointed.

Look at each specific ministry environment and agree on its purpose.

• Who will use this environment?

Will children use this structure? adults? Should it contain "manly" accents because men will be its primary users?

Who will show up for the retreat, the prayer breakfast, the weekend service? Men? Women? Will everyone there be a Christ-follower? What are their stories? Are they likely to be similar?

If you plan a service, a group gathering, or an event of any kind without asking these questions, it's likely people will wonder if they really fit in that environment.

• What do we want people to experience?

What do you want people to feel in this environment? Should the environment be warm and inviting? Should it engender curiosity? Do you want people to feel at home? How relaxed do you want people to feel? Should they feel safe?

What about talking: Do you want them to feel free to talk, or should they understand from the environment that they're there to listen?

Go deeper. Do you want them to feel hopeful? afraid? encouraged? challenged? cared for?

- **What do we want people to leave with?**

Are you hoping people will resolve to do something as a result of their experience? Do you want them to wrestle with a specific question? What kind of steps might they take from here? Is there a natural on-ramp or choice of on-ramps you want them to consider?

- **Who's responsible for quality control?**

After answering these four questions, someone needs to be responsible for implementing the answers. In the case of a new physical structure, a number of people would, ultimately, monitor the quality.

People who understand physical space, relational interactions, and the intended experience must work together to achieve the optimal outcome. This may be a couple of people or several teams from various departments. In any case, someone must be responsible for planning, execution, and follow-up.

Remember the Four Spaces

At Granger we examine every environment through the lenses of the four spaces: public, social, personal, and intimate. Here's how we do it.

1. Public Space: Think "Crowd"

Regardless of the size of your church, you have crowds. Not compared to a church on the other side of town, perhaps, but compared to other gathering spaces in the life of your church, some venues are more heavily populated than others. That would be your crowd. For most churches that's your weekend service. You may see 10,000 or 50 at your weekend services, but if that's the largest gathering, it's your public space.

Here are our responses to the five architect questions when we consider our public space, our weekend services.

What's the purpose of this space? The space is designed to help every attendee experience the wonder, power, and grace of God. More specifically, it is designed to allow people who don't know Jesus personally to explore the claims of Christ, comparing his agenda with the culture's popular views on pressing matters related to relationships, perceived success, fears, and mortality. It's a space to which Christ-followers are comfortable inviting their friends, neighbors, and families, knowing they'll be treated with respect and grace. At the same time, Christians are challenged in this space to integrate spiritual transformation into their own lives and relationships. To achieve these purposes, the space is designed to be safe, warmly inviting, personally accepting, exceptionally positive, and still somehow unpredictable. Safe, but not routine. Positive, but challenging.

Who will use this environment? Men, women, and youth (middle school–aged and older). We intentionally create this environment with the youthful, middle-aged, successful, married man in mind. As we make this space appealing, even captivating, for him, we expect every other demographic will fit.

What do we want people to experience? The specific feelings we hope our guests and members experience will vary from service to service and even from moment to moment within a service. For instance, a specific element in the service may be developed, not to invoke a new feeling, but to lift to the surface a feeling or question listeners have encountered before so they can consider it in light of Scripture and God's invitation to them.

For example, in a marriage series we might explore the issue of trust and the consequences of losing it. So we might use a song such as Bruno Mars' 2010 hit "Grenade" to evoke emotions connected to betrayal, secrecy, and trust. Or we may project video images of grandeur and wonder while singing "Holy, Holy, Holy" to help people experience awe and worship.

We want to help our people feel safe during each service. For many that means "Don't make me talk to anyone I don't want to talk to." So we set up rows of chairs, facing forward, allowing our guests to focus on what's happening at the front of the room. While we do encourage people to briefly greet others during the service and the room is filled with conversation before and following services, this space allows people to be as anonymous or as known as they wish.

We want people to feel that they belong, that this is "their church." To that end, we intentionally create a space where people can explore deeply personal questions at their own pace. We hope they will feel emboldened and challenged to take a step from where they are—wherever that is.

We intentionally create a space where people can explore deeply personal questions at their own pace.

What do we want them to leave with? We always want people to leave with a short menu of potential next steps. We offer a limited number of on-ramps to opportunities that will allow people to take a variety of specific steps they may be challenged to take. For instance, during a marriage series, there could be scores of potential next steps for various couples within a service. A husband may need to step away from an emotional attachment at the office. A woman may need to step toward her husband sexually. A couple may need to establish a regular date night for conversation and romance. But the specific environment we may offer as a next step could be a marriage seminar. Within that space, an individual or couple will have the opportunity to further wrestle with personal next steps and, we hope, be emboldened to act on them.

Who monitors the quality of the environment? At least a couple of teams measure how well we've achieved our goals in this public space. (I'll explore measurements more in the next chapter.) The first group to review quality is made up of the senior pastors, the speaking pastor, the worship leader, and representative technical leaders (audio, video, camera, and so on). Their review occurs immediately after our first service on Saturday evenings. Everything—the flow of elements, timing, content, clarity, and delivery of the message—is reviewed and carefully tweaked. Several days following the weekend service, the entire arts and programming team debriefs each element, reviewing execution and impact.

If the message was unclear because of the arts or the spoken message, we need to address the problem. If there's a chance people were distracted from hearing from God, we need to eliminate the diversion.

Certainly you may host other events or gatherings that create public space. A midweek service, a community concert, or festival may bring together a variety of people who don't have a lot in common but have assembled around a common purpose. Take responsibility for these environments by asking the architect's five questions. In doing so you'll meet your responsibility to the people who will occupy these public spaces.

2. Social Space: Think "Conversation"

At Granger the majority of our other environments are social spaces. Although the people in those spaces initially may not know one another, they have more in common than the people in the public space. They may all be men; they may all be women. They may all want to improve their personal finances. They may be interested in forming groups that will allow them to meet new people.

We apply the same five questions as we develop these spaces. We want people to select acquaintances or initiate friendships there. The agenda or program is designed to not only allow for conversation, but also to create it. We want people to feel safe, but because the participants have more in common than in the public space, more discussion is programmed.

Therefore, we set up social spaces very differently from public spaces. The seating configuration may be around tables. Food and beverages will likely be available. We want people to have a memorable experience that results in tangible, doable next steps that lead to life transformation.

Examples of social-space events include topical seminars around issues such as finances, marriage, or parenting. Affinity-based retreats that extend over a weekend are social-space events with great opportunity for personal space interaction. All-church Bible studies are another example of social spaces at Granger.

3. Personal Space: Think "Time"

Personal space and social space often overlap. The primary distinction lies in the level of trust that has been formed between two or more people. Most often, time is the single factor that allows people to move from "friendly" to "friendship." While this cannot be programmed, leaders can be trained to cultivate conversation that invites personal sharing as a group of people become more trusting of and with each other.

Most often, time is the single factor that allows people to move from "friendly" to "friendship."

We train group leaders to develop environments that are

- *friendly,* where people can get to know one another. The challenge is for each individual in the group to be genuine rather than guarded. However, being genuine doesn't mean dismissing necessary personal boundaries. Forced intimacy is not the goal; being real is.

- *compassionate,* where people can experience acceptance. Compassion is not about practicing tolerance, or merely "putting up" with one another. Rather, we encourage the kind of acceptance that acknowledges that others have intrinsic worth right where they are.

- *caring,* where people can discover that they matter. Even within personal space, no one has permission to try to "fix" anyone else. Rather than "fixing" someone, we seek to provide spaces that encourage personal transformation, which is the work of the Holy Spirit. As people learn simply to listen, they convey great caring. When people take time to understand, they typically exchange judgment for genuine concern. Over time people will ask the advice of people they trust. They will give permission to those same people to ask questions that keep them centered on their personal goals.

4. Intimate Space: Don't Think About It

That may sound strange, but I urge you to ignore intimate space. Just leave it alone. My point is this: Don't try to program intimacy. Don't attempt to create an environment for it, and don't expect it to develop in all group relationships.

For instance, in a mixed-gender group (married or single) of 6 to 12 people, some details about some topics should never be discussed. The illusion that all the people in a circle of friends are equal confidantes is the reason confidences are broken, judgment separates, and groups explode.

Intimacy is the result of deep trust that has been established over time between two people. Remember, most of us will experience as few as five intimate friendships in a lifetime, and half of those will be with family members. Intimate relationships are

Intimate relationships are a product of the Holy Spirit's work in the lives of two people who decide with a lot of tests over time to keep taking risks to trust.

a product of the Holy Spirit's work in the lives of two people who decide with a lot of tests over time to keep taking risks to trust.

You cannot create environments that will automatically lead to this level of trust. This does not mean that the Holy Spirit cannot create a surprising friendship that leads to intimacy from a social or personal space. It simply means we cannot promise it or plan for it.

A Word About That A-Word

Quite honestly, I've come to hate the word *accountability*. For such a long time in the church world, it's been used as a license to browbeat fellow Christ-followers. In the name of "speaking the truth in love," we've portrayed truth as rigid commands delivered with any attitude but love. We've somehow forgotten that the truth also includes the facts that all people matter to God, Jesus died for us while we were still sinners, and we all carry wounds that need to be healed and sins that need to be forgiven. Instead, accountability has taken the form of self-righteous sword-swinging that has left many wounded Christians bleeding and alone, disillusioned with church, Christianity, and Christ himself. Far too often "accountability" is a display of pious, pharisaical judgment wrapped in a repulsive cocoon of spirituality! It angers me.

Friendly, compassionate, caring relationships are not necessarily void of accountability. But I prefer to redefine accountability as friendship. It's a word Jesus used. "I no longer call you servants, because a servant does not know his master's business. Instead, I have called you friends, for everything that I learned from my Father I have made known to you" (John 15:15). Jesus spoke into an ancient culture in which the Jewish people lived under Roman rule, but he stepped out of the hierarchical construct of the world as they knew it. Jesus could have used words such as *king, boss,* or *ruler* to describe himself and terms such as *servant, subordinate,* or *slave* to describe his followers, but he didn't. In his letters, Paul later referred to the supremacy of Christ as Lord, as the ruler of all. However, Jesus intentionally used the word *friends* to describe his relationship with his followers. While it is appropriate, even necessary, to submit to the lordship of Christ, Jesus gives us a model of human relationships that doesn't place one person over another in our journey with and toward God.

> Jesus gives us a model of human relationships that doesn't place one person over another in our journey with and toward God.

According to Joseph Myers, accountability that is nurturing and healthy between friends is "not about catching someone. It's not about keeping track. It's not about laws. It's about finding health—the health that grace and a gentle spirit can bring about, through the compassion of Christ."[5]

Within healthy friendships people can be reminded of "whose" they are. They can be called forward to embrace the desires of their own hearts. And when this is done by a friend who compassionately cares, it will not look like the soul-piercing accountability that too many Christ-followers have endured. It will more closely resemble the friendship Jesus defined.

North Point's Model

Andy Stanley and his team at North Point Community Church have built their ministry on a similar model. But instead of talking about public, social, and personal spaces, they use rooms of a house to describe relationships.

Instead of public space, North Point thinks of the weekend service as a *foyer*. Similar to your front porch, it's a place you would first meet someone arriving at your home. Because they're your guests, you're hospitable. And if you treat them well, they'll likely return.

The *living room* is the room to which guests would naturally migrate if you invited them into your home. This is social space. You might offer them a glass of lemonade (or sweet tea in Atlanta) and invite them to sit with you for a visit. Here they see pictures of your kids, get some insight into your personality through your decor, and get a feel for your home. In this space conversation may turn to shared experiences and similar tastes, and a new level of warmth may be reached. A friendship is developing.

North Point's *kitchen* represents the place where everyone in the *family* wants to hang out. Food is always present. And the exchange is personal. This is where North Point develops their group environments.[6]

Call your environments public, social, personal, or name them after rooms in a home, but be responsible for them. Create them purposefully, honoring the relational wiring God has built into every human being. Be an environmental architect.

Endnotes

1. "David Rockwell Has a Lot of Nerve," fastcompany.com/magazine/node/45800/print.

2. Tim Keel, *Intuitive Leadership: Embracing a Paradigm of Narrative, Metaphor, and Chaos* (Grand Rapids, MI: Baker Books, 2007), 33.

3. "The Seven Axioms of Yves," fastcompany.com/node/60531/print.

4. Thom S. Rainer and Eric Geiger, *Simple Church* (Nashville, TN: Broadman & Holman Publishers, 2006), 26.

5. Joseph R. Myers, *Organic Community: Creating a Place Where People Naturally Connect* (Grand Rapids, MI: Baker Books, 2007), 143.

6. North Point Community Church, northpoint.org/adults/index/C54.

Applying the Architect Questions to Three Spaces

Environment (weekend service, midweek activity, small group gathering, class session, etc.):

_____

Type of Space (circle one): **Public   Social   Personal**

As you develop new environments or evaluate existing ones, ask:

1. What's the purpose of this space?

2. Who will use this environment?

3. What do we want people to experience?

4. What do we want them to leave with?

5. Who monitors the quality of the environment?

From Chapter 5

Your Local Church

■ Summarize the DNA of your church in five or fewer bulleted comments. Ask others from your team or group to do the same. How well does your church understand its DNA?

■ Review the relational environment axioms (pp. 67-68). Evaluate how you're doing with each of these. What could you give more attention to? What additional questions do you need to ask? Who needs to be part of this process?

■ Duplicate the "Applying the Architect Questions to Three Spaces" chart (p. 78). Complete a chart for each venue in your church; then consider how to alter each of them to create environments that best help your guests experience God in the context of human relationships.

■ How have you communicated "intimacy"? How will you deal with false expectations for intimate relationships? How will you appropriately define and communicate about them?

Your Personal Life

■ Think about the environment you've created in your own home. How are your relational values manifested there? Are there ways your family and guests could better experience your values? What changes would that require?

■ What false expectations have you had with various environments at your church? How could you assist others in experiencing each environment's determined outcome?

■ How have you been hurt or helped by "accountability" relationships? How do you "speak the truth in love"? How do you want others to "speak the truth in love" to you? Is there any relationship in which you tend to play "lord" rather than friend? Read John 15:14-17. How could you apply Jesus' words to your relationships?

■ Remember those intimate friends you listed in the last chapter? Call them or send them a note this week, letting them know how their trust and acceptance have influenced you. Tell them what it means to you to be a part of those friendships.

6

How Full Is Your Menu?

"Limit confusion between you and your customers by limiting and refining the choices you present to them."
—*Scott McKain*[1]

I Just Want a Taco

Occasionally I like to visit a local Mexican restaurant. As I scan the menu, I search for items I've never tasted. However, I often feel a little overwhelmed by the menu, which gives me pages and pages of options. There are sections categorized by meat: pork, chicken, shredded beef, ground beef, side of beef. There are pages dedicated to types of food: tacos, enchiladas, tostadas, burritos, flautas, gorditas, nachos, quesadillas, sopes, and tamales. (Hungry yet?) The list goes on and on. Then of course, there are the chef's featured items that can fill another page or two.

Don't get me wrong; I love variety. I love the adventure of trying new foods, but even I feel overwhelmed by so many choices. I'll bet I'm not alone in my typical response after 15 minutes of reading the daunting menu. I typically look up at the server and ask, "What do you recommend?"

Often the server responds, "I don't know what you're hungry for. Do you like beef, pork, red sauce, white sauce, corn, or flour?"

Then I put my decision totally in the server's hands and ask, "What do you like?" Decision made. I use both hands to give the encyclopedia back and wait for my surprise. My wife is the opposite: If the menu is too extensive, she'll simply ask for what she knows and hope it's on the menu. Typically the kitchen is accommodating.

Many of us would complain if the menu were too limited. We want choice; we equate it with freedom. We believe it's our inalienable right.

Conversely, many of us would complain if the menu were too limited. We want choice; we equate it with freedom. We believe it's our inalienable right.

People Want Freedom

With a reasonable grasp of history and the luxury of many more chapters, I could illustrate humanity's rational as well as desperate pursuit of freedom throughout the ages. Since I have neither, I'll just state the obvious: Every human being wants to be free. We want to exercise our gift of free will. In our attempts to find freedom through our power to choose, however, we often create for ourselves and others a reality that is anything but liberating.

Of course nothing threatens our sense of liberty more than believing we have no choice, no options. At its core the desire for freedom honors our Creator's intention: to create through choice, to relate to our world and others through choice, to understand loving relationship through choice. A feeling of "being stuck" breeds hopelessness and a denial of what it is to be fully human.

So we insist on choices. And more choices. Doubt that? Take a stroll through your local grocery store and count the variety of cereals, salad dressings, or soups. We do want choices. No doubt about it. But we are inundated with options.

In 2000, Sheena Iyengar of Columbia University and Mark Lepper of Stanford University evaluated the impact of such a wide variety of choices. A specialty grocery store in Menlo Park, California, offered 24 flavors of jam under one brand label. During week one of the study, shoppers were offered the opportunity to taste any one of the 24 flavors. During week two, shoppers could taste only 6 of the 24 flavors, although all 24 were still available for purchase.

Only 3 percent of those consumers who were given the option of tasting all varieties made a purchase. Amazingly, when customers were given the option of tasting only six flavors, sales hit nearly 30 percent.[2]

This study along with others suggests that when people are given too many choices, they are less inclined to choose anything at all.

You and I experience this all the time.

And so do the guests, attendees, and members of our churches.

The Menu at Church

Ever opened a church bulletin and played 52-Card Pickup? I have. Colored fliers from every conceivable ministry fall to the floor: short-term mission trips, Sunday school classes, family picnics, small groups, the new message series, the building program, a comment card, student ministry, a blood drive. It's not a bulletin; it's a catalog; it's an encyclopedia!

Through these fliers, we hope to achieve many goals. We hope that

- people will be well informed and able to make decisions about where and how to be involved in the church (and most churches are hoping the answer will be "all of it").

- people will see what the church is doing and begin to share its vision.

- people will eagerly step into one or more of the options, and the church staff will be validated.

Instead, the results more closely mirror those in the Menlo Park grocery store. Turnout is poor, effort seems wasted, and people's lives remain uninfluenced.

In his book *The Paradox of Choice*, Barry Schwartz lists a number of consequences of our seemingly unending array of choices. Chief among them is that we tend to be less satisfied with our decisions. In fact, we often regret them, a phenomenon commonly known as buyer's remorse. Ultimately, our pleasure in those decisions flat-lines.[3]

When we offer too many options, most people simply don't choose. *If* they do make a choice, they often don't follow up because they begin to doubt that their choice was the best way to spend their time and resources. After all, there were so many choices. How can

> When we offer too many options, most people simply don't choose.

they be certain they chose the best one? Ultimately people can become dissatisfied because their expectations for near perfection left them disappointed and disillusioned.

The Church Menu Isn't the Only Menu They're Reading

While our people are perusing the dozens of choices we're pushing, they're also making choices about who and when and how to date or marry; their kids' sporting options; how to get everything done in their jobs; purchasing, maintaining, or remodeling their homes—the list is endless.

So while we're encouraging people to join a small group, attend a marriage seminar, or participate in a membership class, they're often not connecting our list of options to the list of decisions they're already trying to make. They're merely adding our list of options to their already overwhelming list of demands on their time, resources, and energy. The result is a crushing burden of choices that may lead to dismissing the church's options altogether.

As leaders we must carefully and strategically consider how to help our people integrate all their choices so that they live out God's kingdom on earth. Otherwise we risk encouraging our people to continue living life in chunked categories where church and spiritual development have little to do with marriage; raising kids; work; or prioritizing time, resources, and energy.

As leaders we must carefully and strategically consider how to help our people integrate all their choices so that they live out God's kingdom on earth.

Examine the way your church talks about the choices it offers. What if you intentionally talked about next-step options as though they really connected with the decisions people are already trying to make?

- Does the marriage seminar answer the questions people are already asking? Say so. Enter that conversation and offer the seminar as a potential part of the journey they're already on.

- Does the membership class tap into your attendees' longing for significance by belonging to something bigger than themselves? Say so.

- Does the invitation to a group experience intentionally connect with your people's hunger for friendship? Then make that connection in the way you talk about it.

When we make an announcement, print a promotion, or mail an invitation, our people ask the same thing we all ask when presented with one more option for expending our time, energy, and resources: "So what? How does that help me right where I am?"

You're offering Sunday school, small groups, sporting programs, women's ministry, membership classes, cookouts, camping trips, missions experiences, Bible studies, shopping trips, and a weekend service. So what?

I challenge you to scrutinize every activity on your church calendar and ask, "So what?" Use the chart on page 86 to assess your strategy. Ultimately, you'll be assessing your strategy. If activities have been thrown on the church menu because "every church" has them—ask again. What are you hoping people will gain from each experience? Among all the choices people face, which steps do you believe would be *best*—not merely *good*— steps to take?

As you answer these questions, you'll begin to narrow your church's menu, allowing people to make reasoned decisions to belong and grow.

I challenge you to scrutinize every activity on your church calendar and ask, "So what?"

"So What?" Assessing Your Strategy

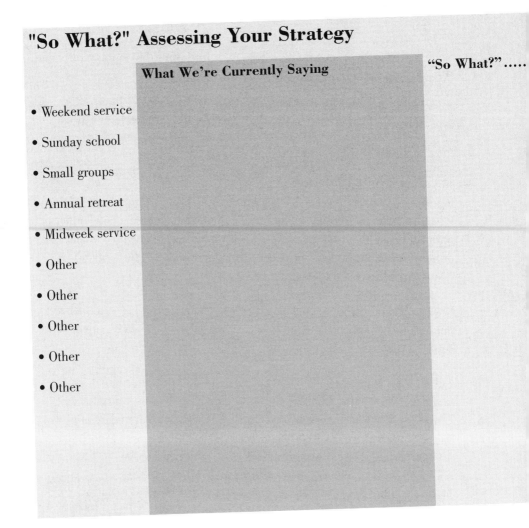

What We're Currently Saying	"So What?".....
• Weekend service	
• Sunday school	
• Small groups	
• Annual retreat	
• Midweek service	
• Other	
• Other	
• Other	
• Other	
• Other	

Making the Menu Effective

Several years ago our senior management team spent our annual planning week asking, "What practices would make us stronger as a church and as individuals in the next 12 months?" Working through *7 Practices of Effective Ministry* by Andy Stanley, Reggie Joiner, and Lane Jones, our senior team as well as many of our department teams began to implement these practices as we evaluated our offerings:

- We asked, "What's a win for us as a church? for our people? for each team? How do we help our people identify a win so we and they know we're actually on mission?"

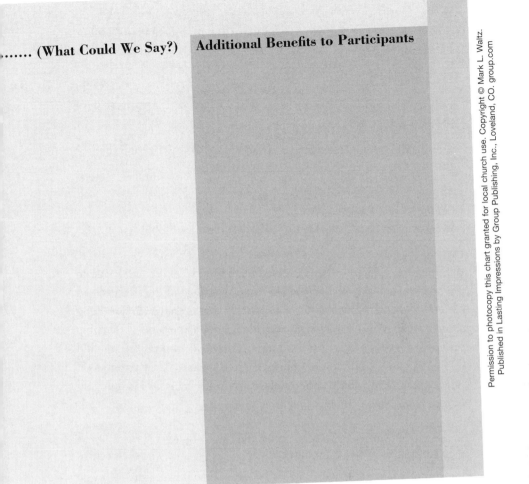

- We asked, "How do we help our people take steps toward God, rather than just take part in an activity?"

- We reviewed our menu and began to sharpen our focus.

- We examined our teaching strategy and asked, "To see greater life change in our people, could we focus our teaching on fewer concepts?"

Implementing these four practices alone has helped to sharpen our mission to "help people take their next step toward Christ...together." (Andy and his team list three more practices to enhance ministry effectiveness. I recommend you get the book, devour it with your team, and work diligently on the process of becoming more effective.)

I'll talk about some of these outcomes more in subsequent chapters, but here's the quick list:

- We eliminated our affinity ministries.
- We simplified on-ramps and narrowed our menu in the weekend experience.
- We revisited our key teaching focus and prioritized scriptural themes.
- We designed seminars, workshops, and events to be natural next steps from our teaching and mission focus.

1. We Eliminated Our Affinity Ministries

At Granger we took two years to become "specifically more generalized" by eliminating ministries that were redundant in time, effort, and focus. In 2003 my team and I began the painful process of evaluating the effectiveness of affinity ministries, such as those for women, men, singles, and married couples. Each of these ministries provided group experiences, teaching events, and retreats. And they did a great job. Every ministry was led by high-capacity leaders who led phenomenal teams. They understood their mission. They put together great opportunities for new people and existing members to connect and grow.

But each team was trying to accomplish the same objective for a different group of people. What would happen if we charged leaders who were experts at groups to help us with groups? What if volunteers and staff who understood the dynamics of a successful retreat planned all our retreats? What if event planners planned events for adults, not specifically for men, women, singles, or married couples?

Ultimately, we asked, "What if we simplified our focus on connecting adults? What if our mission to 'help people take their next step toward Christ…together' streamlined our ministries to all adults, rather than the natural end of most affinity ministries: to plan a great affinity *program* and, from that, a full *calendar of events*?"

We realized that the duplication of effort had resulted in a very extensive menu for our people. Do the simple math. Each of the four ministries planned

- a monthly gathering (4 ministries x 12 months = 48 ministry events),

- small group opportunities (4 ministries x large number of groups = huge number of group opportunities), and

- at least one retreat each year (4 ministries x 1 retreat each year = 4 annual retreats).

Of course, each of these highly functioning ministry teams expected the church to promote each group, event, and retreat. That meant four or more promotions per month and several promotions throughout the fall and spring. If each of these events were printed in the weekend program, announced from the platform, and promoted in the weekly e-newsletter, decision paralysis would result. People would delay choosing, not choose at all, or question their decisions almost as soon as they were made. It was just too much.

You see, although the women's ministry in your church is targeting only women and the men's ministry is targeting only men, unless you have an unusually high number of singles (as is the case in some larger cities), you're often targeting the same families. And as you do, you're targeting the same shared family calendar and budget. If a married woman is deciding whether to attend your women's retreat, she's not deciding alone. Her decision affects her husband and kids. If several family members in one home each have a crucial choice to make from the church's menu of next steps, that can add up to a lot of commitments, even if there's only one offering for men, women, and youth respectively. Add to that offerings from a singles or married couples ministry, and every man and woman is now faced with competing options. Every adult is male or female, single or married. Even two affinity events offered in a single month create a dilemma for every adult in the room.

In 2012, we revisited this human dynamic: People want to connect by gender and lifestage. So we have connection opportunities for women, men, singles, and married couples at Granger. However, they are now offered on a more limited menu. Our ability to offer next-step events or gatherings in conjunction with a weekend series has been improved— without complicating the calendar with too many choices.

We're offering ways for groups of men and women to meet respectively for life journey. We're keeping the options limited but sustainable with effective leadership.

We host large gatherings for men and women to connect with God and one another. However, these events are scheduled, planned, and promoted as a first step from the weekend with options for additional discipleship tracks from there.

2. We Simplified On-Ramps and Narrowed Our Menu in the Weekend Experience

Two groups read your weekend bulletin or program cover to cover. Only two: your newest guests and volunteers and staff who are hoping the events they've planned are publicized there. That's it.

We finally accepted that fact and began to print our program accordingly. This shift also helped us limit the menu on the weekends. If you visit our website, GCCwired.com, you'll see that a fair number of events, groups, and Bible studies is available to our people. It's not as if the menu is sparse. However, the way we promote these options looks quite different in the weekend service.

Our desire is to offer primary on-ramps that allow anyone experiencing the weekend service to take a next step toward Christ. These next steps are limited to four to six options on any given weekend. If a person wants to meet friends and build connections, we provide an on-ramp that will help. Someone who wants to volunteer will find one or more on-ramps toward that objective. Often the weekend message will outline a next step—an on-ramp—toward community, growth, or serving. That particular on-ramp will be printed in the weekend program, limiting the menu so people can choose without confusion or regret.

3. We Revisited Our Key Teaching Focus

Andy Stanley says it best: "All Scripture is equally inspired...All Scripture is *not* equally important."[4] Some churches would argue this point, insisting that their approach to preaching through the Bible, cover to cover, honors the Scriptures, the authority of the Bible, and the God whose story is contained in its pages. Granted, different churches have different approaches to reaching different audiences. However, I believe Stanley's point is affirmed by Jesus' own words in Matthew 22:34-40:

> *When the Pharisees heard how he had bested the Sadducees, they gathered their forces for an assault. One of their religion scholars spoke for them, posing a question they hoped would show him up: "Teacher, which command in God's Law is the most important?"*
>
> *Jesus said, "'Love the Lord your God with all your passion and prayer and intelligence.' This is the most important, the first on any list. But there is a second to set alongside it: 'Love others as well as you love yourself.' These two commands are pegs; everything in God's Law and the Prophets hangs from them"* (The Message).

At Granger we are committed to addressing culturally and relationally relevant topics from a biblical perspective. Topics such as parenting, marriage, friendships, justice, finances, fears, the workplace, and sexuality will be part of our teaching cycle every couple of years. Throughout these series, we will point to God's faithfulness, forgiveness, grace, and purposes. We will contrast our self-seeking agenda with the self-denying agenda of the kingdom of God, inviting people to take their next steps toward a God who says they matter.

We're committed to keeping our focus laserlike in order to increase our effectiveness in *helping people to take their next steps toward Christ...together.*

4. We Designed Seminars, Classes, and Events As Next Steps

Again, I'm not urging you to mimic Granger's approach (or that of any other church) point for point. However, if you are going to apply any of the core principles here, you'll do well to recognize some underlying assumptions in your own ministry. For example, your teaching must address the life issues your people already care about. That is, your teaching must be relevant. Tim Stevens' book *Pop Goes the Church* is completely devoted to the quest of incorporating pop culture into our delivery of the timeless message of God's truth. Speaking of Jesus, he states:

> *If Jesus physically entered twenty-first century America, I believe he would do much as he did in the first century. He would hang out with normal people in the real world, and he would reserve his*

strongest words for the entrenched religious leaders who love their traditions more than they love their people. He would leverage the culture. He would read our books, go to our movies, watch our TV shows, look at our magazines, and surf the internet so that he could better understand our culture. I believe he would look for themes in our popular culture that would help him make a connection between the topics that had our attention and the kingdom life he was offering. He would be encouraged by the lyrics in some of today's mainstream music. He would see honest searching in the words, and he would use those lyrics to reach and penetrate hearts.

I believe that is what Jesus did and that is what he would do, and I believe he expects no less from us.[5]

When our teaching connects real people with real life, then the invitation to use an on-ramp from the weekend service is more than a ploy to make our programs successful. Rather, we invite them to take a step that is naturally connected to the desires and longings that brought them to church in the first place. And when they accept the invitation, they're taking their next steps in the direction of the kingdom of God.

You can offer a tremendous lineup of choices to your people, but if those choices don't connect the message of the gospel to the real needs and concerns of your people, the choices are merely announcements of church programs and activities. That's a lineup that most people have little interest in or time to entertain. They'll choose, all right. Just remember, "no thanks" is a choice.

From Chapter 6

Your Local Church

■ Scrutinize the past three months of your church calendar. How many weekly options existed for family units? If one person were to attend every event targeted to him or her, how many times would that person be away from home? If the majority of your people could participate in only two events each month, which events on your three-month calendar would you choose? How will you prioritize your church events and ministries to accomplish a menu of the "best" rather than an abundant offering of the "good"?

■ Complete the chart on page 86, retyping it to include all your ministry offerings, if that's helpful. How will this exercise help you recalibrate the way you plan each ministry event? How will it affect promotion? Based on this review, what ministries will you eliminate, downsize, or repurpose? After you've completed the chart, rank the offerings from the most important to the least important.

■ Review your weekend message series and messages over the past 12 months. In what ways did you offer clear, tangible next steps? What opportunities did you miss? How could you approach your message planning in relation to next-step environments in the coming 12 months?

Your Personal Life

■ Scrutinize your personal calendar. What choices does your schedule reflect? What level of disappointment did you experience once your calendar was set? What control do you have over the menus you choose from in the coming year? in the next month?

■ Consider your personal motivation for participating in meetings, services, workdays, and other events at your church. How compelling is your answer to the "So what?" question when applied to each? Look at your schedule for the coming week. How might your approach to those experiences be different if you placed God's kingdom agenda (to be more like Jesus, to love God with all you are, to love others as Jesus does) to each one?

Endnotes

1. Scott McKain, *What Customers Really Want: Bridging the Gap Between What Your Organization Offers and What Your Customers Crave* (Nashville, TN: Thomas Nelson, Inc., 2005), 143.

2. Sheena S. Iyengar and Mark R. Lepper, "When Choice Is Demotivating: Can One Desire Too Much of a Good Thing?" (Journal of Personality and Social Psychology, 2000, Vol. 79, No. 6), 996-997.

3. Barry Schwartz, *The Paradox of Choice: Why More Is Less* (New York: HarperCollins, 2004), 119-120, 145, 167-169.

4. Andy Stanley, Reggie Joiner, and Lane Jones, *7 Practices of Effective Ministry* (Sisters, OR: Multnomah Publishers, Inc., 2004), 124.

5. Tim Stevens, *Pop Goes the Church: Should the Church Engage Pop Culture?* (Indianapolis, IN: Power Publishing, 2008), 19-20.

What Do We Expect?

I Don't Always Know What I Need

In the spring of 2008, with a green light in my favor, I made a left-hand turn across three lanes of a fairly busy thoroughfare near the 80/90 Indiana Toll Road. I didn't see the Pontiac GTO that hit me, but I heard the crash, and I felt the impact. Milliseconds later, disoriented, enveloped in the dust of deployed airbags, facing southbound off the road, I knew two things.

I was alive. Good.

I was hurt. Not good.

The EMT asked, "Do you want transport to the hospital?" I thought about it. I was sore. The right side of my torso felt really bruised. I asked the EMT for his best guess. Based on his visual inspection, the fact that I seemed to be breathing OK (What, as opposed to *not* breathing?) and had no external bruising or puncture wounds, he left the decision to me.

So, gasping because breathing was painful, I said, "No. I don't need transport to the hospital." I signed off on my refusal for a trip to the emergency room and stood up (oh, that hurt). I limped back to the wreckage that once was my car and met my friend Tim, who had come to drive me home. (My wife was out of town caring for her parents.) That's what I thought I needed—just to get home.

It hurt to get into the car. It hurt to put on my seatbelt. Tim drove cautiously, but I felt every turn. It hurt to get out of the car, step onto the porch, and sit down again.

"You need anything? You need me to take you to the hospital?" Tim pressed.

"No. I'm fine."

My wife talked with me more than once on the phone, urging me to go to the hospital.

Three hours later, after dozens of friends had called and sent Facebook messages, text messages, and e-mails (people were amazing!), my friend Kent called and asked me to promise to call him for "transport" to the hospital if I was feeling worse in the next hour or two.

"Sure," I promised.

No less than 20 minutes later, Kent was in my driveway along with our friend Jenn. She was there to stay with our daughter, Olivia, and Kent was there to take me to the emergency room. Kent didn't force me into his car, but he was insistent, and I was ready. Three hours after the accident, I was in no less pain. It still hurt to breathe, laugh, and move. Three hours after that, after half a dozen X-rays, CT scans, and blood work, I learned I had four broken ribs and internal bruising.

I hadn't immediately known what I needed.

Sometimes my wife and friends know what I need before I do. What's that about?

Do We Ever Know What Someone Else Needs?

My friend Tim wasn't negligent. He asked. He offered to take me to the hospital. But he had no way of knowing how I felt. He had no experience in diagnosing broken ribs or internal bruising. He asked me what I needed and accepted my answer.

Kent wasn't necessarily a *better* friend to me because he insisted on taking me to the hospital. He's an insurance agent and has seen lots of medical diagnoses. He had enough experience related to my condition to point me in a specific direction.

How do we know what our people need? Can we know? Is it up to us to know?

At Granger we work hard to respect people. We design weekend series and services around topics that address common needs and frequent conversation in our culture. People have needs in their friendships, marriages, dating, sexuality, parenting, finances, fears, hopes, work, and perceived spirituality. We believe God speaks through the Bible to each of these areas of life. So we lean into those topics. We raise questions, we explore common beliefs, and then we juxtapose all of that with God's take on these issues. That's what people need.

But it's not *all* they need. If they think God is merely a great fixer-upper, for example, we've failed them.

So every time we explore our people's needs within their marriages, we have the opportunity to paint a picture of marriage as God designed it. When we address financial chaos and burdens, we can talk about the supremacy of God as Creator and owner of everything. We are able to invite people to rethink their ideas of success and join with God to redeem and restore his creation. Each time we address parenting, we have the privilege of introducing the heavenly Father who loves us right where we are but loves us too much to leave us there.

I thought I just needed the throbbing pain of my right side to go away after my accident. I really needed a trip to the hospital, prescription meds, and lots of rest.

That said, I believe that more often than not, people show up at our churches more aware of their souls' need for God than we may think. Author, scholar, and futurist Brian McLaren suggests that people in church as well as individuals we are trying to reach are asking, *"Can your church help me experience*

That said, I believe that more often than not, people show up at our churches more aware of their souls' need for God than we may think.

God and experience personal transformation?" He continues, "By this question, they're telling us they don't just want to learn *about*. They want transformation. They want to learn Christ."[1]

Our people may think they just need the pain to stop, the confusion to go away, the empty to fill up. Or they may know what we know—they need a relationship with almighty God. So at Granger that's our message week after week after week. And with that message we offer pathways to help them continue their journeys toward God. How those pathways are offered has grave consequences.

The Used-Car-Salesman Approach

At a car dealership, you've experienced the closer, haven't you? You know what you need for your family, for the type and amount of driving you do. But that doesn't matter. Not to this salesman. He knows he needs to move the green Buick that's been on the lot five days too many.

Regardless of what you say you need, he has a counter proposal. And every time it's the green Buick. For every reason you give that you need something else, he has a justification for ol' green. He can't listen. He has one agenda: his.

Sometimes the local church behaves in much the same way. While it's true that our mission is to introduce people to Jesus and invite them to follow him, sometimes our agenda gets in the way. I've worked with well-meaning churches who gave their guests little or no choice about their next steps. The church decided that every new and returning guest must be signed up for the next Bible class or small group, regardless of the needs the guest identified. In fact, not unlike the used-car salesman, some churches sell their Sunday school, midweek service, or small-groups program as the end-all solution to any and every stated need.

The All-Skate Corporate Approach

I don't have fond memories of skating rinks. Generally the memories I have involve bruises and clumsy apologies for taking other people down. No, I don't skate well. I certainly preferred the call from the DJ for "couples' skates." At least then I knew that Laura (yes, she's the only girl I skated with until we had a daughter) would help keep me upright. Most of all, I dreaded the "all-skate" call. That was when everyone hit the floor at the same time. Everyone, at the same time. Time for bruises and apologies.

Church camp seemed to operate much the same way, only without skates. I actually have some positive memories of church camp during my teenage years. It was where I first met my wife. Camp was all about friendships, recreation, chapel services, and sugar binges. There was a printed schedule, and it was enforced. Everyone participated in everything. We all got up at the same time, ate at the same time, went to chapel together, played ball together, watched *Thief in the Night* movies, and bunked down at the same time. Everybody. Same drill. No exceptions. It was an all-skate. There was one good reason. Everything had been thoughtfully planned. Every camper's experience would be maximized if everyone participated.

At one time at Granger we had a similar approach. Every environment was designed thoughtfully and prayerfully—services, groups, Bible classes, retreats, all of it. We heavily promoted every activity and program. We said something like this: "If you're following Jesus, you ought to be serving somewhere; you should be evangelizing your neighbors and friends and bringing them to church services with you; you'll grow at the midweek venue fashioned for believers; you should be in a small group; you should dedicate time to your family."

A survey revealed that we were asking our people to cram nine days of activity into a seven-day week. We had set up a no-win scenario for our people. Our approach ignored work schedules, personalities, preferred pathways to God, and individual next steps. We had unintentionally communicated, "Our mission is to take every step at the same time in the same way toward Christ."

On the weekends we were quoting Jesus' words to our new guests: "Are you tired? Worn out? Burned out on religion? Come to me. Get away with me and you'll recover your life. I'll show you how to take a real rest. Walk with me and work with me—watch how I do it. Learn the unforced rhythms of grace. I won't lay anything heavy or ill-fitting on you. Keep company with me and you'll learn to live freely and lightly" (Matthew 11:28, The Message). But once our people were "in," we might as well have been quoting from Ecclesiastes 2:23: "All his days his work is pain and grief; even at night his mind does not rest. This too is meaningless."

Balancing the Tension

At Granger we backed up and changed two things: our expectations and our promotions.

In revising our expectations, we acknowledged, for example, that some people work second shift; they will seldom, if ever, attend a midweek event. We accepted that we were still a church *with* small groups; not everyone would participate. We agreed that there were preferred pathways to help individuals grow in their relationships with God. Not everyone would or could take the same step at the same time.

Changing our expectations immediately affected how we talked about the various venues available to connect, serve, and grow.

"Many of you will find Bible study in our midweek service to be a tremendous benefit to your journey with Christ."

"Some of you would like to meet others here at GCC in order to grow in your trust in Jesus. Starting Point is a next step you might want to explore."

We've heeded the advice of Chip Heath and Dan Heath: "If you say three things, you don't say anything."[2]

And as my wife says, "Sometimes more is just more."

We've decided not to dictate next steps for our people. We've opted to respect them and trust the Holy Spirit.

But We Do Have an Agenda

Regardless of your church's structure, it undoubtedly has an agenda. For most of us our agenda includes bringing people into personal relationships with God and helping them develop as revolutionaries in God's here-and-now kingdom. We don't exist merely to form nice community clubs or self-promoting social networks. We have a clear agenda.

Since 1986 when Mark Beeson, his wife Sheila, and their three children planted Granger Community Church, we have had one mission: *"Helping people take their next step toward Christ...together."* Mark has assembled a team that shares his commitment to the Greatest Commandment (Mark 12:29-31) and the Great Commission (Matthew 28:18-20).

Since the late '90s we have structured our teaching, staffing, and environments around the five key characteristics found in the Greatest Commandment and the Great Commission.

- We need *connection* with God and others.
- We must *grow* in our relationship with God.
- We are created to *serve* out of our God-designed wiring.
- We must *reach* our community and world with Christ's love.
- Our lives are to be lived in full surrender to God, which is our *worship*.

Our agenda is clear. We want our people to connect, grow, serve, reach out, and worship. That's what it is to partner with God in bringing "up there" "down here." That's it. We want to help people get there.

Focusing the Agenda

In 2011, after a two-year journey involving our entire congregation in a five-year visioning process, we embarked on our 2016 Vision. With the Great Commandment and the Great Commission as our foundation, we committed to "Raise the BAR" as a church in the following ways:

Be the Church: *The number of people being the Church in their neighborhoods, schools, cafés and communities seven days a week will outnumber the number of casual Christians just going to church.*

Our vision calls for every person to live out their God-given mission right where they are, every day. One's ministry is not limited to the four walls of the church building, although many will find an expression of their ministry in a volunteer team. Every person has a missional impulse to care, to reach, to influence a cause, to love a group of people. Every person already resides and works within a societal domain: justice, education, healthcare, government, religion, business, and the arts. Our call by Christ is not to merely go to church; we are to be the Church. Every day. Right where we are.

Activate the Campus: *We will have remodeled the Granger campus and programs to help not just our congregation, but the greater community, with Jesus at the center.*

Our pastor of Life Mission and co-author of *Missional Moves*, Rob Wegner, has observed that many churches merely exist in a city, some are against their city, but Granger Community Church will be for the city. We do not want to merely be a church building where people gather on the weekend. We want to see our area transformed in Jesus' name, and we want to utilize our buildings to do that.

We want our restaurant and atrium area to be a go-to place for people in our community—not only our congregation—to gather for conversation and shared experiences. We want our neighbors on the property, walking their dogs, exercising, and yes, seeking God. We want our community to know this is a space for them.

Reproduce at Every Level: *Every follower of Jesus will be a reproducing follower of Jesus. And every church will be a reproducing church.*

This is a canyon-sized leap from a guest's first weekend experience at Granger. But it's our unapologetic prayer. It's our vision for their soul. It's our agenda.

We're rethinking discipleship. It's a vibrant, exuberant, adventurous journey, but it's not merely a stroll with Jesus. It is followership. It means we go to the kinds of places Jesus goes. It means we love the people Jesus loves. It means we center our lives around his character, his agenda, his priorities. Discipleship means we reproduce. Each of us. All of us. Every person. Every campus. Every congregation.

This vision is God-sized. And it is individual-ized. That is, we'll only accomplish this vision by the power and leading of almighty God. And we intend for every individual to be transformed in the process. It will mean our people learn to connect and build healthy relationships. Each person will be invited and challenged to serve—in our formal ministries or in their community. All of us will need to be students of Scripture and in deepening relationship with our Father. Our marriages, finances, parenting, leadership, relationships, sexuality, habits, and time will be transformed through obedient steps as disciples of Jesus.

The tremendous challenge is to cast this God-sized vision while living in the tension of personal choice. People can only be where they are. They decide their next step. Our call is patiently love, while persuasively inviting.

> There is a tremendous risk that our returning guests and often our church members will mistake our agenda for our end goals.

Focusing the Agenda in Your Culture

The point, again, is not to cut and paste our vision to your church like a plug-and-play program. What outcomes honor Christ's commands and fulfill your vision of ministry in your church and community?

Remember the "so what?" Our 2016 vision has helped our people figure out *their* next steps. Clearly these goals represent what we believe is God's agenda for our lives. Hence, they are our agenda as a church. However, these objectives are not a destination. There's no point at which any person in our church can announce, "I did it. I got in your group, I've taken your classes, I've served on your teams, I've reached out through your missions program, and I've worshiped." Anytime I've heard a Christian talk this way about his or her experience with God or church, this statement usually follows: "So what?"

There is a tremendous risk that our returning guests and often our church members will mistake our agenda for our end goals. Do our guests think our goal is simply to increase the number of people participating in our programs and activities? They will if we fail to tell them why participation is important.

Consider the "so what" our people hear as we call them to step into our 2016 vision:

> *You are the Church right where you are. Your significance is not found in completing any series of activities at church. You are the Church. Your purpose is not to score perfect attendance at church. You are the Church. Your life is not to be discovered*

and lived as a church-goer. You are to go every day, where you are…be the Church.

Your story matters—to God and to others around you. We live our lives on mission so that we fulfill God's potential for our lives. So we experience real life. So we live out who he made us to be.

Each of our campuses is to be shared with our community. This is space not to hide, but to be known. A space not to merely be served, but to serve others. This space is a tool for you to extend an invitation to your neighbors, coworkers, family, and friends so they can experience people who are real and caring. People who accept people right where they are.

God wants more for you than for you to know the Bible. He wants you to experience dynamic relationship with the Jesus of the Bible. He wants more for you than for you to understand Christian dogma and doctrine. He longs for you to embrace the grand stories of the Bible, stories of God's creation, exodus, restoration, and redemption. God wants more for you than for you to get by. He wants to reproduce your life in another life, evidence of emotional and spiritual health as a disciple. God wants you to be alive!

The "so what" matters. Vision is the "why." Say it clearly. Help your people take steps of intentionality toward a destination, not merely a stop at the next church program.

Provide Structure to Your Newest Believers

I met Vicki in a group designed to help people explore their places in God's story. The group wasn't limited to new Christians or Christ-followers at all, although most of the members felt very young in their growth. Vicki's story intrigues me, partly because it's so different from my own and partly because I'm hearing more and more similar stories.

Vicki went to Sunday school and church as a child. So as she was growing up, she wasn't unfamiliar with God or the Bible. But, deciding church was irrelevant and boring, she stopped attending church as a teenager. She showed up at Granger Community already on her journey toward God.

Her path had taken her through Buddhism, the Baha'i faith, and other Eastern religions. Interestingly enough, she found some enlightenment along the way, and it led her back to an evangelical, Christ-centered church.

She beamed one night in our group conversation because she had just learned about "The Top 10," an upcoming study on the Ten Commandments being offered through our midweek gathering. The series was promoted like this: "Thirty-five hundred years ago, Moses came down from Mount Sinai with a list that has shaped the hearts and values of people and nations ever since. We know them today as the Ten Commandments. But do we really know—let alone understand—them? Join us as we explore common misconceptions about the Ten Commandments to reveal the role they can play in our lives today."

Vicki exclaimed, "I'm so excited. I've been praying, wondering what my next step is. I just wanted to know how to live, what to do. And then I learned that this series is starting soon. I'm so excited!" Although this series was for everyone at Granger, she perceived this as *her* very next step in *her* journey.

Our midweek offering has changed several times over the years as we have traversed the various seasons, requiring new approaches to developing people as disciples. Our menu of next step on-ramps from the weekend service generally include:

- Discovering GCC—our orientation and membership class designed for people exploring our church, the claims of Christ, or both.

- The Table—a secure, GCC-only online landing for prayer, sharing items and services with our faith community, and connecting in groups.

- Volunteering—offered as an invite to explore options online, participate in a VolunTOUR, or check out our Volunteer Expo.

- Affinity connections—from MOPS to men's Bible studies to large-group, single-evening events designed to help people connect meaningfully with same gender or life stage peers.

- Spiritual formation venue—a short-term, group-based class designed to help us engage our vision and personal steps in our relationship with Christ.

These few opportunities provide a limited, structured pathway to next-step environments, clearing the clutter of too many choices while allowing freedom to choose one or more in any order. We fiercely protect these tension-creating values in our church culture: intentional, structured venues that help our people take specific steps toward Christ *and* complete freedom for the individual to choose what those steps look like.

Our ends remain constant. The means are always changing. There are no sacred cows when it comes to methods or environments. The format of weekend services may change, midweek services might be altered, more classes might be developed, online communities will be enhanced. There's a good chance that more than a couple of environments will be different when this book is published or re-released.

Don't try to mimic Granger's next-step environments or North Point's gatherings or Willow Creek's small group strategy. If you do, that model will change with time anyway. Develop spaces and opportunities that allow your people to explore their faith and to experience God in genuine relationships—in the context of your church's DNA and culture.

Experience and surveys have shown us that one type of these paths is chosen more often than others. We'll zero in on that in the next chapter. Keep reading.

From Chapter 7

Your Local Church

■ In what ways might your church be assuming it knows what everyone needs? What are the all-skate, cookie-cutter approaches that may be alienating some people in your church? In what ways is your church playing the used-car salesman? How could you help people see God's agenda for their lives without rubber-stamping a rigid pathway for everyone?

■ If you haven't already done so, prioritize the top three to five practical outcomes you want for your people. How will you communicate them? How will you support their journeys? How will you clearly answer the "So what?" question?

Your Personal Life

■ What activities have you tried to copy from someone else's journey? How effective were they in developing Christ's character in you? How have you personalized practices and disciplines so that you own your steps and subsequent growth?

■ Where in your personal growth do you need to "raise the bar"?

Endnotes

1. Brian McLaren, "From Information to Transformation," Leadership (Summer 2005), 104.

2. Chip Heath and Dan Heath, *Made to Stick: Why Some Ideas Survive and Others Die* (New York: Random House, 2007), 33.

8

Develop Relational Road Maps

"It's not candles but community, not art but attitude, not liturgy but love that makes a difference in our broken world."
—John Burke[1]

Small Groups: Of or With?

Are you a church *with* small groups or a church *of* small groups? I remember first hearing this question in the late 1980s. For more than 20 years, the question has apparently had only one right answer that has largely gone unchallenged. How you view small groups will influence everything you do to connect people in relationships and help them grow; hence, common wisdom has dictated that every church should be a church *of* small groups.

The only part of this conclusion we've agreed with at Granger is the first part of that last sentence: "How you view small groups will influence everything you do to connect people in relationships and help them grow." We've chosen to answer the next part differently. We've chosen to be a church *with* small groups.

There's one reason for this decision. In fact, we've already talked about it. People can only be where they are. They can only take a step from where they are. And not everyone at Granger is ready to join a small group. I'll bet they aren't at your church either.

We believe in relationships. How we go about helping people prioritize and practice relational living is a matter of methods.

Get this. Small groups are a method. A good method, but still a method.

In some churches, adult Sunday school class is still a method. In others, Sunday school and small groups are methods. Other churches use home groups, cell groups, life groups, house churches, Bible study groups, or interest groups as methods for accomplishing the goal of small groups. They're all methods.

And the method isn't necessarily wrong. In fact, many churches have studied Acts 2:42-47 and concluded that small groups are biblical. We've studied this same passage and concluded that *relationships* are biblical and small groups are an effective way to help people enter and cultivate life-transforming relationships.

As you answer the question *"of* or *with?"* you determine how you'll focus and what you'll communicate. If you determine that you'll be a church *of* small groups…

- you'll expect everyone to be part of one.

- you'll elevate the importance of this step over most other steps at your church.

- people may feel that other steps don't have much significance compared to the step of getting into a small group.

- people may hear that if they're not part of a small group, they're not meeting the church's expectations.

You may be a church *of* small groups. The truth is many of the churches I most respect (for a variety of reasons) are churches *of* small groups. Furthermore, the objectives we want for our people—as a church *with* small groups—are the same that these churches *of* small groups want for their people.

- We believe that biblical teaching is a catalyst for life change and that life change best happens in relationships.

- We believe that experiencing grace—unconditional acceptance—in personal relationships often opens the door to receiving God's grace.

- We believe that our people are best cared for by the people with whom they are in relationship.

- We believe that people will "stick" in the local church as they connect with others.

- We believe serving is best practiced as a team, a joint effort with others with whom we share mission and relationship.

However, how all this gets communicated is subtly different, depending on your church's answer to the question *"of* or *with?"*

I'm not on a mission to see churches cancel their small group ministry. I'm not even bent on changing your paradigm. I am intent on asking you to *review* your paradigm. Consider *how* you communicate. Ask some questions, and look for honest answers about the *effectiveness* of your strategy.

There was a time in recent history that nearly every local church had a Sunday school ministry, not only for children, but also for adults. In many churches that program has changed into a small-group ministry. I won't be surprised if someday in the not-too-distant future more than a few churches begin to transition from small groups to a different relational environment. I don't know what that might look like, but given that small groups are a method, they're likely to change.

If or when that change comes, we want our people to continue to invest in relationships—whatever the method, whatever it's called.

So continue your small groups, house churches, or cell groups, but teach, preach, and encourage relationships. And remember, people will take their next steps from wherever they are. For many that step will be to connect in a group. For others it will be to return to a service next weekend or to participate in a social-space event.

Encourage people to take *their* next steps. Encourage next steps that are highly relational.

> I'm not on a mission to see churches cancel their small group ministry. I'm not even bent on changing your paradigm. I am intent on asking you to *review* your paradigm.

Spiritual Friendships With People Who Aren't Christians

What did you think as you read the above heading? I'd bet the farm you immediately thought *evangelism*. I want to help you expand your thinking. While it's true that we encourage our people at Granger to invest in the lives of friends, family, neighbors, and work associates who don't know Jesus and invite them to check him out in a weekend service or another relational venue, that's not what I'm talking about here.

What if I suggested that Christ-followers can be encouraged and challenged in their journeys with Christ by intentionally involving themselves in personal relationships with those who don't claim to follow Jesus? Is it possible that we'd rethink our assumptions and discover something new about God? Can the spiritual questions and observations of non-Christians help us grow?

I believe so.

Look at Acts 10. The story is a case study about how a Christian's faith can be challenged by someone whose spiritual experience doesn't stack up to our "informed" standard. Cornelius was a captain of the Italian Regiment. The Bible tells us that "he was a devout, God-fearing man, as was everyone in his household. He gave generously to the poor and prayed regularly to God" (Acts 10:2, NLT).

Hit the pause button.

> The point of the story is that Cornelius, a Gentile, is about to be used by God to smash Peter's (and the other apostles') theology about the kingdom of God and its inclusiveness.

I used to think this passage suggested that Cornelius was a Christian. But that's just sloppy reading. You see, he didn't know the truth about Jesus, the Messiah. Christians, properly defined, are Christ-followers. The point of the story is that Cornelius, a Gentile, is about to be used by God to smash Peter's (and the other apostles') theology about the kingdom of God and its inclusiveness. There are plenty of people in our society who "fear God" and give generously to good causes.

Some of them are celebrities with no known connection to a church; some of them are people in our communities who read the most recently Oprah-endorsed book; and some of them are people who are checking out our churches but don't necessarily follow Jesus. We can imagine no good reason to embrace such people as Christians. Peter likely considered Cornelius in the same light.

Cornelius was not Peter's idea of a Bible study companion. In fact, Peter may have initially thought Cornelius fell into the group that Paul was referring to when he said, "Don't become partners with those who reject God" (2 Corinthians 6:14, The Message). As I was growing up, this verse was used as a harsh mandate to have nothing to do with "unbelievers" because they would only pull me down into their God-hating, conniving bent toward evil. However, the wording of this passage in The Message clarifies a distinction that's easy to miss in other versions. It's one thing to compromise our faith in God in order to build a spiritual alliance with someone who rejects the truth about God; it's another thing entirely to come alongside someone who's not convinced but open to exploring spirituality and truth. That's the distinction to which Peter is introduced in Acts 10.

God revealed to Peter that he had misunderstood the inclusiveness of the good news. It really *is* for everyone. No exceptions. If you keep reading this New Testament story, you'll come to verse 28, where Peter says to Cornelius, "But God has shown me that I should no longer think of anyone as impure or unclean" (NLT).

Human beings—Christian or not—have God's image stamped all over them. Human beings matter to God, whether they are aligned with our theology or not.

So what does this have to do with helping people connect relationally in our local churches? It means that we include everyone. Yes, everyone.

- **Affirm your seekers' reflection of God's image in their lives.**

I've never known anyone whose experience with God started only *after* attending church. Although people may not have recognized that God had been active in their lives, after attending church services for a short time or meeting Christ-followers, they began to connect experiential dots and were able to trace God's hand in drawing them to him.

I've heard pastors speak to or about non-Christians in their weekend services as though everything about their lives was vile, God-hating, and destructive. Of course when the message follows that God changes us into new creations, these people are confused. What about the charity, goodwill, and kindness they've always displayed? It would make much more sense to tell people they're invited to leverage their hearts, which are already formed in God's image, for a different cause—the cause of God's redemptive kingdom in the world. What if our weekend crowd heard us say what Peter said to Cornelius? "God has shown me that I should no longer think of anyone as impure."

People matter. Right where they are.

• Invite people to serve—now.

Create opportunities for people to volunteer, to make a difference with their lives just as soon as they are willing. We'll explore this more in Chapter 9, but for now consider this: Why tell people they can't serve until they've become fully devoted followers of Jesus? Isn't it confusing to encourage people to join Christ's work in the world through serving, then add that it really doesn't count unless they're believers?

• Involve anyone in small groups.

Don't segregate "seekers" in their own group conversations. Their questions are often no different from those of new Christ-followers or even of Christians of long standing. Unfortunately, many of the latter have stopped asking questions. Long ago they accepted the dogma others told them. Now that dogma is mere information that may or may not produce Christ's character in their lives.

When group conversations involve people with varied levels of understanding and experiences with God, everyone learns. Seeking, unconvinced people tend to ask questions that jolt staunch, settled-in believers out of their complacency. Conversely, believers who thoughtfully share their spiritual experiences can open seekers' eyes to God's work in their lives.

Don't Reject the Value of the Journey

I talk with a lot of church leaders who fail to see the value of journey. They seem to feel that once people have heard the truth, the only thing left to do is to obey. After all, Jesus said, "Then you will know the truth, and the truth will set you free" (John 8:32). So they think, "You want to be free, you want to live life to the full? Then hear the truth and obey. Period."

But it's never that simple.

I often ask church leaders with such immediate expectations for discipleship to consider their own lives: "Have you always been mature in your faith? What step have you taken recently in your understanding or practice of your faith? How long has it taken you to get where you are today?"

Those who are willing and able to honestly reflect on the incremental nature of their growth sheepishly admit, "It's taken me a very long time to really accept and practice what I've known cognitively for most of my life. I'll probably learn more tomorrow. I'm not yet who I'm going to be."

When we're honest about our own experiences, we realize our faith has taken *years* to develop. Our journeys have been composed of many relationships (with Christians and non-Christians alike), good experiences, horrible ones, learned practices, interaction with the Scriptures, and a growing willingness to give our lives to others. We've not always been where we are today. We've had numerous "you are here" points along the way. And from any given point, we've been able to take our next steps only from that place.

I grew up in the church, but I didn't understand grace until I hit rock bottom and found myself confessing my entire life to a few intimate friends. I've claimed to be a law-abiding citizen, but not until my daughter began driving did I really change my driving habits. I've not always been where I am. Some of the steps I've taken have been the result of many faithful steps over time. I've fought and resisted some steps until I had no other choice. And each time I've had to take my next step from where I was.

> **W**hen we're honest about our own experiences, we realize our faith has taken *years* to develop.

Our people need to learn to trust us and those around them. They need to chat over a bagel and a cup of coffee to begin to realize that people are genuinely curious about them.

And yet we're so tempted to expect others to share our current X. We must realize once and for all that they can't. It's not only improbable, it's impossible. They can only take the next step from where they are.

Sharing the Journey Is About Trust

Our people need to learn to trust us and those around them. They need to chat over a bagel and a cup of coffee to begin to realize that people are genuinely curious about them. They need to learn for themselves how a grace-filled relationship can be life-changing. They need to journey through a myriad of life experiences to learn to connect the dots between biblical truths, their own misperceptions of God and self, and their need to serve and be served.

Church can't be reduced to a trip with a travel guide monotonously pointing out static truths. Rather, it must be embraced as a journey that includes personal experiences, connecting the past with the present, the present with the future, the Bible with life, and people with people. The picture of the kingdom is about process: the growing mustard seed (Matthew 13:31-32), the wandering child whose journey leads him back home (Luke 15:11-32), the woman who searches every inch of her residence until she finds the lost coin (Luke 15:8-10). Jesus says the kingdom is open. It's inclusive. And again and again he describes it as a process, one step after another, a journey. Always relational. Always with others.

We are created to be in relationships with others. People who keep returning to your church will do so because they find relationships there. Those who don't find meaningful relationships will either leave or continue to be silent observers from their Sunday morning seats.

Barriers to Taking Steps Into Relational Spaces

At Granger we've discovered some barriers that prevent people from stepping into relational environments, such as groups, right away. You've probably experienced similar hurdles in your setting:

- "I'm at a unique place in life. No one will relate to my situation."

- "Small groups are for Christians. I'm not sure what I believe yet."

- "I don't understand the Bible. I'd be the laughingstock of the group."

- "I've heard about small groups. They last forever. You can't get out of them."

- "What if I don't like anybody there? They're probably all weird."

- "I've never prayed out loud. What if they ask me to pray? I'd rather die."

- "All I want are some friends, some familiar faces. I'm not ready for 'deep.' "

- "I've heard that people air their dirty laundry there. My business is my business."

- "How small is a small group? I won't be able to hide."

- "The last group I was in was the Parent-Teacher Association. That meant paying dues, boring meetings, and fundraising. No thanks."

People are afraid. How do you help people push past their fears into relationships?

- **Address relational barriers with fresh labels.**

This is new for us at Granger, although we've been trying to apply a safe label for small-group relationships since I joined the staff in early 2000. Plenty of churches have successfully relabeled their small groups, helping people enter into these relational environments.

- Lakewood Church in Houston, Texas; Life Pointe Church in Homestead, Florida; Living Hope Church in Vancouver, Washington; and Overlake Christian Church in Redmond, Washington, call them *life groups.*

- Mars Hill Church in Seattle, Washington, refers to small groups as *community groups.*

- Oakleaf Church in Cartersville, Georgia, has *journey groups.*

- Northway Church in Malta, New York, features *connection groups.*

Each of these churches has worked to remove barriers to social- and personal-space relationships by attaching a new label to small groups. Change it up. Get creative.

> **N**othing communicates as well as a story. That's what makes the Bible so compelling. It's a grand story of stories.

Or do what we did. Drop small groups.

We've discovered what most of the churches above have discovered: *Small groups* is a churchy phrase. Who else besides churches have small groups? Hardly anyone. Hence the stigma and the fears associated with them.

People understand groups. They're just... groups, groups of people. New people to Granger don't have to wonder what they're joining when they participate in a group. It's simply a collection of people heading in the same direction for a season.

Some groups at Granger are designed around friendships (MOPS), others are focused on growth via emotional and spiritual health (Bible studies), other groups have a volunteering focus (every serving team), and still others are centered on life stage or topical conversation intended to help people apply truth to their lives. But every group is predicated on the supposition that relationships are key to connecting, growing, serving, sharing, and worshiping.

- **Address relational barriers with stories.**

Nothing communicates as well as a story. That's what makes the Bible so compelling. It's a grand story of stories. It's what we enjoy about a good movie or television show. We sing along with ballads because of their stories. That's why several times each year at Granger we dedicate an entire weekend service to storytelling—not from the pastor, but from our people.

I'll never forget the weeks leading up to the weekend when Josh was going to tell his story. Since Josh had moved to town from Texas, his praying aunt had encouraged him to address his sense of purposelessness and loneliness by going to church. He'd found our church simply because he lived across the street from our campus...and because the Holy Spirit was at work in his life.

The only people in town he'd met were Cody and Katie, neighbors who had become friends over beer binges and card games. One night Josh set his beer down, looked at his friends, and asked, "Want to go to church with me in the morning?"

Cody had no frame of reference for church; he'd never been. Katie had only bad memories of judgmental, narrow-minded people. But Josh was their friend. If he was up for it, they'd give it a try.

Katie didn't feel judged at Granger. In fact, she felt these people were genuinely caring. Cody loved the band. And Josh left feeling hopeful. His aunt was ecstatic.

After several weekends they stepped into a class led by our senior pastor, a class designed to help attendees explore our church, our faith, our purposes, our mission, and our vision. In that class these new friends heard the good news that they'd been hearing every weekend: They mattered to God. Jesus had come. He'd demonstrated God's love through his life, death, and resurrection. He'd brought God's kingdom to earth, and they were invited into it. They were invited to follow Jesus from this point on, from their X.

They said yes.

That experience led them to take a step into another group session designed to help them explore their faith and establish practices that would help them get to know Jesus better. There they discovered other friends their age. Nearly half of them were fairly new in their journeys with Christ; the others had been committed to Jesus for some time but were new to Granger.

They decided to get together. All eight of them.

Over the next several months, they celebrated the birth of one couple's baby, they read the Scriptures together, they shared questions and struggles, they observed birthdays, and some of them traveled to Las Vegas with Katie and Cody to witness their wedding. They learned to experience life together and took organic steps that weren't outlined by a small-group ministry. Together they discovered that God kept showing up. The Holy Spirit was changing their world.

When we told Josh's story, it wasn't just Josh's story. The entire group was present at all five services to unpack their amazing journey. We didn't outline the common fears we wanted to address for our listening weekend crowd. We just told the story. The fears were addressed, and for more than a few, the door was opened to explore relationships through groups.

- **Address relational barriers with permission
  to experiment.**

According to the Myers-Briggs Type Indicator, up to 30 percent of the U.S. population is introverted, with that number going as high as 50 percent among educated professionals.[2] Consider your church in light of that statistic. If one-third to one-half of your weekend attendees and members are introverted, what should your group environment look like?

Introverted people are less likely to walk into a group of people who have already established friendships with one another. They're less likely to walk into a room filled with new faces and just strike up conversations. They're certainly more likely to shy away from any long-term commitment to a group of people they've not met.

What if your people were allowed to experiment?

No annual commitments. No lifetime expectations. Just a trial. See if the shoe fits. Try it on for size. Experiment.

That's exactly what we're doing at Granger.

- Jump into Discovering GCC. Learn all you can about this church. See if ours is a mission you want to help shoulder. If you want to become a member, this is your step. If not, attend, get your questions answered. No obligation.

- Check out The Table online. Share a prayer request; find the support of others praying with you. Have a need? Post it there. Have something to share or sell? Post it there. Interested in exploring a number of group opportunities—from Bible studies to book clubs to hobby groups? Join one or create one on The Table.

- Find an area or two that seems interesting and volunteer. Experiment. If you don't like it, try something else. But get started. Take a first step.

After that, try as many as you like until you find that team, that area that is fun, engaging, and fulfilling.

- Attend an affinity gathering. Meet some other people who are living life where you're living it. We won't force friendships—only you can decide those—but we'll create the space for you to learn, meet some people, and decide if you'd like to take another step.

- Most of our class offerings are 4 to 10 weeks long. Jump in. You've had jobs you've hated that lasted longer than three months. You can do this. It's short-term. Meet some people, maybe make a friend. Take a step, just for a few weeks.

Andy Stanley summarizes God's calling on the local church as "creating environments where authentic community can take place. Building relational, transforming communities where people are experiencing oneness with God and oneness with one another. Communities that are so satisfying, so unique, and so compelling that they create thirst in a watching world."[3]

How does your church measure up?

From Chapter 8

Your Local Church

- Is yours a church *with* or *of* small groups? How is your strategy helping people connect in relationships? How could your strategy be improved?

- In what ways are your people valued, regardless of their level of maturity or trust in Christ? What opportunities exist for Christ-followers to listen, care, and learn from those who are still unconvinced? What relational environments exist for those who are still unconvinced to build relationships with Christ-followers? How important is this to your church? What benefits might come from this?

- What barriers prevent people from taking steps into relationships in your church? How could you remove those barriers?

- Whose stories does your church need to hear?

Your Personal Life

- What relationships have marked your life in positive ways? Who specifically is most responsible for influencing you in your experience with God?

- What barriers tend to prevent you from forming intimate relationships?

Endnotes

1. John Burke, *No Perfect People Allowed: Creating a Come-As-You-Are Culture in the Church* (Grand Rapids, MI: Zondervan, 2005), 24.

2. clientleadership.com/assets/pdf/client_development_for_introverts.pdf.

3. Andy Stanley and Bill Willits, *Creating Community: 5 Keys to Building a Small Group Culture* (Sisters, OR: Multnomah Publishers, 2004), 45.

9

Construct Volunteer Venues

"Many people believe that volunteerism is more about duty and drudgery than fun and fulfillment. Sadly, sometimes it is."
—Bill Hybels[1]

People Want to Make a Difference

Americans are volunteering by the millions. According to a recent survey, over 62 million Americans volunteered in some capacity at least once for an average of 34 hours in 2010. Nearly 35 percent of them volunteered through a religious organization.[2]

A quick Amazon.com search produced nearly 22,000 different resources on volunteering. Some of those are written with a local church orientation, but many are not. In *Volunteer: A Traveller's Guide to Making a Difference Around the World*, the authors quote Vikki Cole, an international volunteer: "Without sounding clichéd, I really wanted to be able to look back on my life and to have done something of substance that didn't directly benefit just me."[3]

People Will Volunteer Before They Look for a New Friend

In our own survey at Granger, we discovered that when our people take a step to connect or be involved beyond the weekend service, four out of five choose to volunteer with a team rather than joining a small group.

The choices people are making about relationships and volunteering is a fascinating conundrum.

In 2006 researchers revealed an astonishing picture of American friendships. For most Americans the number of close friends dropped from just three friends in 1985 to only two friends in 2004. (This number remained the same in 2010.) People with no close friends at all climbed from 10 percent in 1985 to nearly 25 percent in 2004.[4]

In spite of these startling relational shifts, the 62 million Americans who volunteered in 2010 represent an increase of 3.6 million people since 2002.[5] I believe these statistics validate both the idea that God has wired human beings to want their lives to make a difference as well as the idea that humans are wired to be in relationship with others. I believe the heightened interest in volunteering—in and out of the church—is also a definitive pathway for connection. People want to be part of something bigger than themselves. And they want to share that experience with others.

Task vs. Relationship

Encouraging people to volunteer in the local church isn't merely a way to ramp up interest in or enthusiasm for the church. There's real work to be done. Jesus demonstrated this when he said, "The harvest is plentiful, but the *workers* are few. Ask the Lord of the harvest, therefore, to send out *workers* into his harvest field" (Luke 10:2, italics added). Every volunteer team at Granger has an important task to perform. We're engaged in kingdom work, a movement that requires forward motion from every participant—staff and volunteers alike.

However, if task is all that matters, connection will never happen. In my first book, *First Impressions,* I mentioned that at one time our structure allowed ushers and greeters to show up, grab a handful of programs, distribute them, help with the offering, and go home. A volunteer could serve and experience no community at all. That's a mistake. And over time, it's a mistake that will breed burnout and high attrition rates. Volunteers matter too much. Our new and returning guests matter too much. People matter too much to allow this mistake to go unchecked.

John Maxell writes, "Effective teams have teammates who are constantly talking to one another."[6]

When team leaders are intentional about creating space and contact points for meaningful connection, there is an appropriate balance between task and relationship. An e-mail I received from a volunteer in our church says it best:

> *For me, there is no question that volunteer efforts are one of the best ways we offer to build relationships...The strongest relationships I've built @ GCC have been through the opportunities I get to volunteer. There is something about walking into a room of people that you know share your heart for... (fill in the blank). You don't have to explain why you are there, or what keeps you coming back, or how you almost feel guilty because you feel like you get more than you give. You don't have to worry about them giving you the "God bless you; you're either a saint or a fool" look—they just get it. There is a connection that's made that crosses age, social-economic backgrounds, gender, etc. You connect at a heart level. It's almost like maybe it's part of God's plan!*

Making a Difference Produces Ownership

I've seen it again and again. When people begin to tithe, they have an increased interest in the church's ministries. The same is true of people who invest their energy and time. I've watched people join small groups and Bible studies and remain inactive in the mission of the church. They may love their friends and enjoy the study, but unless they give their money, energy, or time to the church's ministry, they won't feel any ownership of it.

Two Sides of the Door to Volunteering

On each side of the volunteer door are two groups of people: those who wish to volunteer and those who wish they would. Church leaders create and develop programs and ministries that advance the church's mission. Most are aware that they can't achieve their goals without the help of willing volunteers. At this point churches opt for one of several outcomes.

One is to lower expectations and reduce ministry goals. If you accept that the volunteers just aren't available and you can't hire more staff, you set the goal aside. That's certainly one option. And at times saying no to new initiatives because you can't add one more thing to your plate is an indication of healthy boundaries and wise leadership.

Another option is to hire more staff. However, financial constraints rarely allow you to take this step. It also perpetuates the idea that ministry is a function of paid church professionals, which leads to a constantly escalating need for more staff.

Or you could find more volunteers to accomplish the task. Unfortunately, this often results in a frenzied, pressured staff whose sole objective is to recruit increasingly elusive volunteers to assume the increasingly demanding responsibilities of accomplishing the mission.

On the other side of this volunteer door, however, is a host of individuals who desire to make a difference with their lives. They want to volunteer. They wish they knew how and where.

Confronting Common Volunteer Myths

A number of myths prevent people from connecting meaningfully in the local church. Don't assume these myths don't exist in your church, and don't assume they'll go away easily. Identify the myths and get strategic about how you'll debunk them.

Myth 1: "There's no room for me; it's all being done already."

You and I know nothing could be further from the truth. But our people believe it.

At Granger our guests pull into the parking lot, where they are directed by a traffic team to an open parking space. Depending on the distance from their parked car to the building, a shuttle driver will offer them a ride to the front door. There they are greeted by one or more volunteers, who welcome them to the service. A team is ready at the children's check-in area, and campus guides are available if families need assistance finding children's rooms. Friendly teams of people are deployed throughout the children's center and each classroom, and rooms are prepared for each session's activities. Restrooms are clean, stocked, and deodorized.

In the auditorium people are given printed programs, and appropriate seating, lighting, and music are in place. During the service, teams of artists present music, media, and drama. The pastor is prepared with a relevant message.

Every need has been anticipated; everything is covered. "They must have all the volunteers and staff they need," thinks the normal Granger attendee. I would guess that this is a common myth in your church as well. Every staff and volunteer leader knows it's a myth. There's always room for more volunteers.

> **I** consider it a problem if someone in our church boasts of having enough volunteers.

Debunking Myth 1

- *Talk about it.* Address the issue from the platform. At Granger we do this frequently, directly, and simply: "There are abundant opportunities to make a contribution. There's room for you." And then we point to the variety of ways our people can contribute. Don't assume people will figure this out on their own, because they won't. So talk about it.

- *"Chunk" new roles.* In their book *Simply Strategic Volunteers,* Tony Morgan and Tim Stevens use this phrase to describe dividing volunteer projects and roles into several manageable parts. For example, if one volunteer is currently responsible for preparing the toddler space for the weekend, chunk the responsibilities to include more people: someone who washes toys; someone who cleans the floor; and someone who copies, cuts, and collates activity sheets. One person doesn't have to do it all. Chunking roles creates more opportunities for volunteers.[7]

- *Make sure it's a myth.* I consider it a problem if someone in our church boasts of having enough volunteers. If teams can't find ways to involve more people, it may mean they've stopped dreaming, become cozily settled in a "we four and no more" team of friends, or hit a lull in their creative approach to including more volunteers. Only in our band, where there is a limited number of instruments, do we *occasionally* find we have enough volunteers. Tony Morgan puts it this way: "The church can't afford to have 'Not Hiring' signs posted on the front door."[8]

Myth 2: "Volunteering requires too much time."

This myth may or may not be true in your church. If the only way to volunteer at your church is by serving every week for hours at a time, this may not be a myth; it may be an unfortunate reality.

Debunking Myth 2

- *Create First Serve opportunities.* We picked up this concept from Willow Creek Community Church. At Willow, First Serves are "one-time serving opportunities offered at a variety of times and tapping into a wide range of skills and areas of interest." Willow's mantra is "Come once and check it out. No strings attached." People are invited to help prepare the auditorium for weekend services, clean up during services, assist with maintenance projects—one time.[9]

- *Provide a variety of schedules for serving.* Some roles in our children's ministry require 60 to 90 minutes of service each week. Other volunteer roles in children's ministry and almost every other department are needed as infrequently as once a month. Some volunteers—such as our Green Thumb teams, who spruce up and maintain our campus landscaping during the spring and summer—serve on a seasonal basis. Other courageous teams clear snow and de-ice pavement during the winter.

Myth 3: "Volunteering is for extroverted leader types."

People tend to think all weekend volunteers are outgoing and vivacious because they see them on the platform or in guest services or children's ministries. Is there a place for behind-the-scenes introverts? Is there more to volunteering than singing a solo or delivering a dramatic monologue?

Debunking Myth 3

- *Use video to celebrate the variety of volunteer styles in your ministry.* We use video montages set to music to celebrate scores of volunteers at one time. In one 5-minute video, we show smiling faces everywhere, from the stage to the cleaning closet. When volunteers are celebrated regardless of their roles' visibility, we reiterate that there's room for everyone, introverts and extroverts alike.

- *Tell stories.* Use your website, media, blogs, newsletters, and public gathering spaces to give a voice to behind-the-scene volunteers who will never take center stage to tell their stories. For example, we told

Marci's story during a women's retreat after the speaker challenged women to step up and lead as strong women of God. The message was personalized when we talked about Marci's unassuming, faithful role in scheduling and updating our volunteer calendar for over six years.

Myth 4: "Volunteering is only for mild, introverted types."

One of the greatest challenges in the local church is to involve professional, extroverted, type-A leaders in meaningful volunteer roles. While leadership in the kingdom is first about humble servanthood, we must find ways to allow *all* our people to maximize their serving potential by leveraging their personalities, gifts, and skills. Too many leaders—both men and women—have been sidelined because they haven't found opportunities appropriate to their wiring.

Debunking Myth 4

- *Share the responsibility.* Do more than delegate; take some responsibilities off your own plate. Answer these two questions: What are you doing that *no* one else can do? What are you doing that someone else *can* do? The answer to those two questions will allow you to untie the cape from your neck and breathe more easily, as well as empower both another leader and the ministry. Understanding just what needs to be released and accomplished by someone else will create a role description. When a role description has been developed, it's fairly easy to identify a leader to fill that role.

- *Recognize leadership when you see it.* Often you won't have a vacant role waiting for the right leader to assume it; rather, you'll first discover someone with exceptional leadership qualities. Schedule a lunch, connect that leader to another staff leader, and help them explore your ministry mission. Any time leaders are drawn to your church, remember that they're wired for one thing: leadership. We've had some stupendous leaders help park cars and rock babies, but by nature they aren't doers, and they didn't wear the fluorescent vest or burping towel for long.

Becky, a former pharmaceutical account representative, faithfully held babies for months, but our ministry benefited a lot more when she stepped up to lead in our WiredChurches ministry, networking with other ministry organizations and vendors to partner with us for our annual conference.[10] Tom, who manages IT systems and support for our area's largest hospital, still serves with our parking teams and brings systems thinking to our entire parking ministry.

Look for proven faithfulness—evidence from the marketplace or other volunteer leadership roles—among potential volunteer leaders. But often volunteers you'd never suspect to be leaders will prove themselves to be just that—leaders. And when they do, you'll need a plan to engage them. Believe me, your ministry will be better for it.

Myth 5: "Only Christ-followers can volunteer."

I know of some churches in which this is not a myth; it's a hardcore reality. You must be a Christ-follower, be a member, and understand your spiritual gifts before you are allowed to volunteer in any capacity in the church. Not at Granger. Almost anyone is invited to volunteer.

I understand that the work we're doing is kingdom of God stuff. However, a re-read of the gospel narratives may disclose a different portrayal of those Christians who participated in Jesus' life and ministry. The early disciples left their tackle boxes and spreadsheets to follow the rabbi, Jesus, but were they Christians? To what extent did they understand Jesus' plan, motives, and approach? When I think about Jesus' words to Peter, "Get behind me, Satan!" (Matthew 16:23) and the disciples' attempts to restrain children who wanted to approach Jesus (Mark 10:13), I scratch my head and doubt they were all that convinced and committed to the game plan.

God has used braying asses, cunning prostitutes, a womanizing iron man, and thick-headed fishermen to accomplish his work. I don't know why that would be different in our time and culture.

Remember James' observation: "In the same way, was not even Rahab the prostitute considered righteous for what she did when she gave lodging to the spies and sent them off in a different direction?" (James 2:25). God has used braying asses, cunning prostitutes, a womanizing iron man, and thick-headed fishermen to accomplish his work. I don't know why that would be different in our time and culture.

John Burke makes this observation about Gateway's first year of ministry: "Often people were put in positions of service before they found faith…We created many opportunities for involvement serving, regardless of where a person was spiritually."[11]

Will we knowingly allow a womanizing man to lead a greeter team at Granger? Absolutely not. But we would allow him to serve on a number of other teams that limit his frontline access to female guests. He matters to God and has other qualities that can be used in community and service. God created and values everyone. Everyone can make a contribution. And everyone needs to be connected.

Debunking Myth 5

* *How do you see the pathway to God's kingdom?* Do you think of it as an "in or out" proposition or as a journey? I don't have the space here to explore these two contrasting paradigms, but I believe your take on this concept has much to do with how well you'll incorporate every person into a volunteering role at your church. If the Christian experience is a matter of crossing a line—in or out, saved or unsaved—then you may find it difficult to entrust the work of God's salvation to those who haven't yet crossed a line of faith.

  However, if you see the pathway to the kingdom as a journey, there's plenty of room for people at every stage along their journey to Christ. This understanding is captured in our mission statement: "Helping people take their next step toward Christ…together." We believe people have been on their journey well before they ever came to our church. We believe they are seeking, asking, and exploring because in spite of their past relationships with God, they're not currently rejecting him. They're on a good journey. They're taking one step at a time.

  As people who haven't crossed a line of trust yet engage relationally with volunteering Christ-followers, they get to see the claims of Jesus lived out. They are included in prayer, the Scriptures, and conversation that encourages, challenges, and bolsters their next steps toward Christ. If they aren't *serving with us,* then they're not *taking steps with us.* And if they're not taking steps with us, we've failed in our mission, and they're either not taking steps at all or are taking them in spite of us.

* *Acknowledge every volunteer.* Get used to the idea that someone may have seen one of your volunteers slammin' one down in the bar last night. It's about journey. It's about next steps. When I was in high

> If you take on the role of moral police, the jailhouse will be full, and your efforts to rescue the perishing will be reduced to lighting your own little world with your self-polished halo.

school (it doesn't matter how long ago that was), a senior matriarch in my home church said, "The church is a hospital, not a museum." Everyone in the church is a work in progress. If you take on the role of moral police, the jailhouse will be full, and your efforts to rescue the perishing will be reduced to lighting your own little world with your self-polished halo.

Are there standards for leadership? Absolutely. Leaders must be held to an appropriate code of conduct. Leaders must be Christ-followers who share the vision and DNA of the local church. Their lives must be marked by the character of Christ in lifestyle and attitude. I want to see that level of godly influence before recognizing someone as a leader. Influence predicates responsibility.

So I'm not suggesting we dismiss basic requirements for leadership within the church. However, we must value every contribution and life equally. Every person matters, wherever he or she is on the journey.

- *Expect people to trust their lives to Christ* because they experienced his grace as they served. Larry didn't know Jesus when he came to Granger. In fact, he had dropped his wife off for church every week for months. One Easter weekend his Sunday shopping during the church hour was derailed because the stores were closed. Larry found himself in the place he'd resisted most of his life.

That first visit turned into two, then three, then a new weekly pattern. Sundays weren't for shopping anymore; they were for church. Larry hadn't been brainwashed or had his money hijacked by a smooth-talking televangelist, so he felt safe enough to step into an event to serve the community with his wife. That function led Larry to another team where he began to serve more frequently. Those relationships led to a men's breakfast and Bible study. Those relationships and the work God was doing in him through Scripture and serving put Larry on a fast track toward Christ. Today Larry is a growing Christ-follower and a leader of volunteers. His story and love for people are creating a safe place for a shared journey. But it happened one step at a time.

Invite every person who wants to volunteer to jump in, build relationships, and find meaning in serving others.

Myth 6: "You have to know what you're good at before you can volunteer."

I've taken a dozen tests assessing my giftedness. I've used them to help volunteers understand where and how to volunteer. Too often I've witnessed just how frustrating they are for many people, especially people with limited or no previous church background. These folks simply don't know our religious vocabulary and have had little or no occasion to exercise these gifts in the context of the local church. So they tend to check out all together.

Debunking Myth 6

* *Encourage people to experiment.* It's what First Serve is all about. Easy in, easy out. In fact, at Granger we define this slightly differently than they do at Willow: A first serve is an opportunity to serve without making a team commitment upfront. Experimentation is encouraged across all our ministries at Granger. We remind people, "After test-driving a role, you can join the team. Or, if you're not jazzed about it, you can start over and try something else—in the same area or one completely different. The key is to find the place that really fits you."

  Several years ago I stopped a volunteer in the hallway and asked about her experience. She leaned on her mop handle and said, "I think I've served on every team there is in this church. It's taken me years to find what I'm wired to do, but I've found it. I love volunteering on the facility care team!"

  At one time this volunteer had no idea what she might be best suited to do. In fact, like many volunteers, she watched others serving in more "prominent" roles and desired to serve on the vocal team, teaching kids, or greeting guests. But those responsibilities didn't fit her God-given design. With enough experimentation, she found the best fit for her.

* *Choose your words carefully.* Language matters. By now you may have noticed the number of times I've chosen the verb *volunteer* when I could have used *serve*. The word *serve* is prominent in the vocabulary of the church because it's the language of the Bible. However, unless you want to involve only those whose hearts have been fully turned toward Christ, the word *serve* can be a loaded bomb for those not yet convinced or new in their relationships with Christ.

Remember Tyler and Bev? They have been willing volunteers; however, I suspect that their response to the invitation to serve would not have been so eager. "Does serving mean I'm 'in'? I've been assimilated? Does serving mean I'm doing what Jesus did? So, I'm a Christian? I don't think I'm a Christian yet. And I don't want to be assimilated." *Serving* can be a scary word.

But everyone knows what it means to volunteer. Moms have volunteered in their children's classrooms. Men have volunteered as coaches for their sons' baseball teams. Many adults have volunteered to give blood, help with a neighborhood watchdog effort, or distribute bottled water along a marathon route. Anyone can volunteer.

So we choose to capitalize on the most common word. We teach what it is to follow Christ, to learn and live his character, to give our lives away as servants. But when we invite people to serve, we initially invite them to volunteer.

Opening the Door to Volunteer Begins With a Tap-Tap

Although every staff and volunteer leader in every local church at least occasionally thinks the answer to volunteer-recruitment needs lies with the persuasive, impassioned vision-cast of the senior pastor, alas, it does not. In fact, studies show that in and out of the church, more than 40 percent of Americans who volunteer do so because another volunteer personally invited them.[12] Yes, effective volunteer recruitment boils down to personal invitation.

Tim Stevens says that shoulder-tapping, the personal invitation, is the responsibility of every leader and volunteer team member. "I'm not referring to the people sitting next to them on Sunday morning, but the people standing next to them in life—the people with whom they are in relationship." He continues, "It is so inviting to hear, 'Join me.' This tells me that someone wants to be with me, that I have worth, that I can make a difference."[13] Encourage your people to invite their friends to join them in volunteering. Effective shoulder-tapping is key to connecting your people through volunteering.

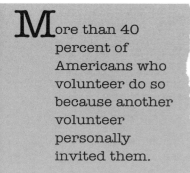

More than 40 percent of Americans who volunteer do so because another volunteer personally invited them.

The 90-Second Invitation

You have about 90 seconds, that's it. If your personal invitation can't be summarized in about a minute and a half, you're not ready to shoulder-tap. People are busy. People are constantly solicited for their money and time, in and out of church. Your invitation to them had better strike a chord in less than two minutes, or you'll lose their interest.

I believe an effective personal invitation has three parts: personal affirmation, a distinct opportunity, and your personal passion for the opportunity. This can't be spin. It's not about being slick. If the shoulder-tapping is perceived as one more sales job, we've missed the point.

- Personal Affirmation—If you were merely recruiting to fill quotas for volunteers, this wouldn't be a factor. However, we're not merely recruiting. Your focus must be on the individual who brings a unique contribution to your church. How will you help this individual become involved in a way that helps him or her build relationships, develop ownership, and take steps with God?

  Verbalize the explicit skills, giftedness, and personality traits you see in this person. Be specific. "I've noticed your gregarious interaction with people around you. I saw how you went out of your way to help that young mom get to the children's center to pick up her daughter. You seem to have a natural, disarming approach to people." Do you think this prospective volunteer is checking out of the conversation? No, she's affirmed. You've noticed her, and you've noticed her for who she is.

- A Distinct Opportunity—The second part is an invitation to explore a specific volunteer area that you believe your friend's uniqueness matches. So you add, "Because of the way you relate to people, I think you'd be in your element volunteering in guest services here at the church. You're already greeting and assisting other guests around you. You're a natural fit on our guest services team!"

- Your Personal Passion—Occasionally I've had a friend or family member hold a forkful of food up to my face and say, "Try this!"

"Have you tried it?" I ask.

"No."

"Then why should I be your guinea pig?" I respond.

I enjoy new foods; it's an adventure for me. But even I feel set up when the dish doesn't come with a recommendation based on personal experience.

Your invitation will yield similar results if you can't support your recommendation with an enthusiastic, personal endorsement. The final part of the 90-second invitation sounds like this: "I volunteer as a greeter in our guest services area, and I love it! I've met some fantastic people on the team; now this place doesn't seem as big to me. Plus, the more I give, the more I receive. I'm having the time of my life!"

In less than 90 seconds you've affirmed your friend, outlined the opportunity, and shared your personal passion. Sometimes that brief conversation may be enough to invite the person to meet a team leader, attend an orientation, or shadow you during a service. Ultimately, the exchange has piqued her interest enough to pursue more conversation. Make it personal. Be affirming. Be specific. Be passionate.

People Matter

When you invite people to personally make a difference with their unique, one-and-only lives, you tap a God-space within them. People are hardwired to be part of something bigger than they are. They want to make a contribution, and they don't want to do it alone. They want to know that their involvement matters. In fact, they want to know that *they* matter.

When people know they matter to God, the transformation of their inner lives is nothing short of a miracle. When people know they have worth, they are most capable of loving God and loving others. When people love God and others, they are obeying the Greatest Commandment. They replace old tapes about their lack of worth with a sense of personal purpose.

> When people know they matter to God, the transformation of their inner lives is nothing short of a miracle.

Kristy had endured a 20-year marriage in which her husband constantly denied her worth and dignity and had affairs with other women. As she volunteered in our church office, we watched her sense of worth blossom. Her new view of God, herself, and others has resulted in a changed life, regardless of whether her marriage is ever changed.

Kristy began to volunteer, and it catalyzed her spiritual growth.

People really do matter. They can make a difference. We must make certain they know.

From Chapter 9

Your Local Church

■ If guests want to connect through volunteering, what strategies are in place to help them do so? How long does that process take? Who's responsible to ensure the system is functioning well and people are making appropriate connections?

■ What is your staff-to-volunteer ratio? Does this ratio reflect your values? Of your weekend crowd, what percentage is volunteering? What percentage is a win for your church?

■ Name the myths about volunteering in your church that you need to debunk. How will you do that?

Your Personal Life

■ How has serving others developed your personal relationship with Jesus? How has it influenced your worldview?

■ How can you personally involve others in serving with you in your church or community?

Endnotes

1. Bill Hybels, *The Volunteer Revolution: Unleashing the Power of Everybody* (Grand Rapids, MI: Zondervan, 2004), 24.

2. Corporation for National & Community Service, "Volunteering in America: State Trends and Rankings" (volunteeringinamerica.gov).

3. Charlotte Hindle, *Volunteer: A Traveller's Guide to Making a Difference Around the World* (Oakland, CA: Lonely Planet Publications, 2007), 118.

4. Jonathan McKee and Thomas W. McKee, *The New Breed: Understanding and Equipping the 21st Century Volunteer* (Loveland, CO: Group Publishing, Inc., 2008), 19.

5. Corporation for National & Community Service, "Volunteering in America: State Trends and Rankings."

6. John Maxwell, *The 17 Indisputable Laws of Teamwork: Embrace Them and Empower Your Team* (Nashville, TN: Thomas Nelson, Inc., 2001), 197.

7. Tony Morgan and Tim Stevens, *Simply Strategic Volunteers: Empowering People for Ministry* (Loveland, CO: Group Publishing, Inc., 2005), 21-22.

8. Ibid, 56.

9. *The Volunteer Revolution*, 71-73.

10. Learn more about INNOVATE, Granger's annual conference to inspire, celebrate, and equip innovation in ministry, at wiredchurches.com.

11. John Burke, *No Perfect People Allowed* (Grand Rapids, MI: Zondervan, 2005), 273.

12. United States Department of Labor, "Volunteering in the United States, 2007" (bls.gov/news.release/volun.nr0.htm0).

13. *Simply Strategic Volunteers*, 45-46.

On-Ramps, Exit Ramps, and Mile Markers

"People don't like stepping off a cliff into the dark; they have to see where the step is before they are willing to take it."
—Andy Stanley[1]

I Can See It, But I Can't Get to It

I've often found myself in a large, unfamiliar city trying to locate a shopping mall, church, or cinema complex. Then I've spotted it. There it is, just ahead on the right. It's big, it's looming on the horizon…and there it goes. I passed it.

I was headed in the right direction. I could see my destination. The road I needed was right there. But I didn't know how to get to it. I couldn't find the exit from the highway or the on-ramp to the road I wanted.

We do the same sort of thing in our churches. We create engaging environments. People are excited about getting together in community. But they don't know how to get there.

Too Many Signs Hide the On-Ramp

On long road trips, our family sometimes plays the alphabet game. You know the one: Everyone reads license plates, road signs, and billboards—anything outside the vehicle—in an attempt to be the first person to locate all the letters in the alphabet. There's a catch. Each letter must be the first letter of a word, with the exception of the letter "x."

As a kid I loved this game, especially in cities. There were countless billboards, so I always had a pretty good chance of finding the elusive "q" or winning the game with the difficult-to-find "z." But as an adult, who is also most often the driver, the game is maddening. More than once, I've missed an exit ramp or an on-ramp because the billboards that were so good for the game were horrible for travel. The road signs were lost in the alphabet soup strewn across the horizon.

You know where I'm headed with this. When our church menu is broad, our people can read all the signs (if they take the time), but too many options can hide the on-ramps to the environments they want or need. Get rid of the clutter. Make sure the on-ramps are clear.

Build On-Ramps to Relationships

For several years at Granger, we experimented with ways to help people make small-group connections. There were groups formed around hobbies, groups doing in-home Bible studies, short-term groups, affinity-based groups—you name it, we had it. Such variety provided great opportunities for people to find their niches. It also created two problems.

First, if our goal was to form a group around every person's interest, our goal would never be achieved. Someone would always be unhappy and feel left out. Jesus didn't do it. He didn't try.

Second, when the number of choices is too broad, at best people will be confused; at worst they'll choose not to choose. When a guest asked how to make connections with friends, no one in our church answered the question the same way. He may have been told about a men's Friday morning breakfast group at a local restaurant. An informed staff member may have directed him to Starting Point. Another equally informed staff member may have shown him the number of groups formed around interests and hobbies. In the end, confusion replaced connection.

Today when someone wants to know how to meet people and connect in a group, there's a simple menu. And everyone—volunteers at our guest services center, staff, key volunteers, and virtually anyone who glances at our weekend program—knows. It's simple and clear.

Build On-Ramps to Volunteer Connections

As I've mentioned, personal invitations through shoulder-tapping are the most effective way to help people volunteer. But if you're teaching about the value of serving at all, other on-ramps should also be visible and accessible.

- **Host an expo.**

Every year or so, we roll out a weekend series at Granger to teach the value of volunteering, of serving. The focus of the series is to help people explore their God-given designs and serve something bigger then themselves: the kingdom of God come to earth. Within that context we offer clear on-ramps to experiment, learn more, and choose an area of volunteering within the work of our church, on and off campus.

A few years ago we moved away from what we called a Ministry Fair to a Volunteer Expo (I'm sure we borrowed the name from another church). We found that the mere label was more understandable and less intimidating for people new to our church or Jesus. This on-ramp shines a spotlight on core ministry areas, illuminating opportunities to volunteer and meet people while doing so.

Here's the simple plan that's worked for us.

- Create stations for key ministry areas and clear signage for each.
- Staff each area with "people people" who have a passion for the area they represent.
- Provide succinct handouts, including a brief profile of the opportunities, the next step, and contact information.
- Ensure that every team follows up within the next 24 to 48 hours, expressing enthusiasm about the step the volunteer has taken and anticipation of their next step together.

Over the course of a few expos, we've also learned what *not* to do, as well as helpful alternatives.

- Don't create space for every volunteer role in the church. The menu will appear too large and overwhelming. Also, don't publicize roles that don't qualify as first-serve opportunities. (You don't want to publicize an option only to take it away.) The more streamlined, the better.

- Don't give teams freedom to decorate their own booths. This can quickly turn competitive as ministries vie for guests' attention. Pretty soon the expo skyline will have so many billboards, balloons, and free trinkets, your guests won't see the on-ramp. Ask your expert design team to theme each station, bringing uniformity and unity to the call to volunteer. It's not a contest. It's an opportunity.

- Don't make the event too time-consuming by encouraging people to visit every station and collect hoards of information. During the service, give people broad-stroke information about general areas. Encourage them to choose only a couple of stations that interest them most and then narrow their choices to one single starting place. After all, a person can only be in one place at a time. There'll be plenty of time and opportunities to experiment, experiment, experiment.

- Don't invite people back for a series of meetings. If an orientation is a logical next step after the expo, be sure to provide a way for people to sign up before leaving so their next step is hands-on.

An expo demonstrates the value of volunteering. Everyone in the church is exposed to the opportunities and catches the vision. Those already serving are celebrated, painting a picture of contagious fun and considerable fulfillment.

- **Host an all-skate serve.**

Each Christmas our people extend our reach into the community through acts of service. We've bought and distributed truckloads of food and personal care products to several food banks and thousands of private residences. In a single Saturday morning, hundreds of people step up to give to our community. It's a massive effort that introduces scores of individuals to the joy of volunteering.

Organizing a first-serve, all-inclusive event at a single time and place allows us to focus on promoting the value of volunteering and of service. That focused promotion not only involves new people, but it also has a significant impact for Christ in our community.

- **Host a volunteer on-ramp online.**

If you visit our website (GCCwired.com), you'll find links to six primary volunteer opportunities:

- guest services and care
- campus support
- missions
- arts
- kids and students
- technical and skilled

These six areas are the same limited stations featured at our Volunteer Expo, and guests are able to navigate the website with the same simplicity and ease they experience at the expo. Plus, potential volunteers can explore connection on-ramps from the convenience of their own homes, offices, or mobile devices. Once they select an option, a volunteer or staff leader initiates a dialogue about next steps.

- **Host a tour.**

Fellowship Church in Grapevine, Texas, offers prospective volunteers a behind-the-scenes peek at volunteer opportunities. At Fellowship it's called Backstage Pass.[2] We've begun a similar tour at Granger, called Voluntour. During a weekend service, we invite people to gather with a small number of other guests for a walking tour of the facility to explore the scores of first-serve volunteering options on and off the campus. The tour makes it easier to choose a place to start volunteering. Within a couple of days, a ministry leader contacts the new volunteers to arrange next steps.

On-Ramps Should Include, Not Exclude

As you systematize on-ramps to belonging, be certain you've chosen language that includes rather than excludes. Believe it or not, words such as *small group* and *serve* can alienate people. Perhaps you've renamed adult Sunday school classes or your student ministries, but if the only way you refer to them is in your church's vernacular, guests will not feel included. They will either miss the road sign because the label isn't clear, or they'll move past it because they feel excluded from the "club."

Remember North Point Community Church's model I described in Chapter 5? I've worked with several dynamic churches that have employed this rooms-of-a-house model and even extended the metaphor. For example, one church identified every event with either the foyer, living room, or kitchen and associated each with the relationship of the persons for whom that space was designed. For instance, the foyer events were for guests, the living-room events were for friends, and the kitchen events were for family members. On one hand, it was a brilliant plan—people felt free from getting in "too deep, too soon." On the other hand, if "guests" wanted to participate in a "living room" event, they felt excluded. The church maintained the room strategy for its ministry, but it wrestled with how to communicate various events so guests always felt included. The church eventually removed all the "room" labels in print and on the website, choosing instead to promote opportunities for connecting and volunteering that would appeal to everyone.

On-ramps must be visible, easily accessible, and inclusive.

Provide a GPS

I'm notorious for getting lost. I need my phone GPS app. Using my app, I can identify my destination and follow the voice navigation system. Plus, if I need a restaurant, tour site, or another stop along the way, I can add stops along my route. Pronto! The interim stop is now part of my itinerary, map included. It's easy to make a stop along the way.

At Granger we've set up some clearly marked destinations: Discovering GCC, groups on The Table, volunteering, and numerous studies. However, guests can plot their itineraries in the order that makes the most sense for them. Their life stage, walk with or toward God, current relationships, and life challenges will determine the steps that are most helpful to them.

Let people own their journeys with God through the relational environments you provide.

Don't Forget the Exit Ramp

When I was in high school, a buddy and I drove from Indianapolis to Cincinnati to check out a college he wanted to see. On the trip to Cincinnati, we made all the correct turns, found all the right on-ramps, and arrived at our destination exactly as planned. On time. No problems.

Coming home was a different story. We followed directions onto Interstate 465, the bypass that loops around Indianapolis. We should have gone on the loop from the east, where we entered, to the south side, where we would exit on Indiana Highway 37. Except we couldn't find the exit ramp. We circled the city no fewer than three times before we finally saw the elusive sign for the ramp that would end our dizzying rotation. (Mountain Dew was our strongest drink, I assure you.)

I've been in churches where the only way to step out of a volunteer role in the nursery was to change churches; to get out of a small group, you had to move to another city. You were expected to be there until you died or Jesus returned. There was no way out, no exit ramp.

> I've been in churches where the only way to step out of a volunteer role in the nursery was to change churches; to get out of a small group, you had to move to another city.

Build exit ramps for every environment you create.

- After a volunteer has experimented with an area of service and decided to make a commitment, be specific about the duration of the commitment. Ask for six months or a year. This actually makes the commitment more meaningful than saying, "Volunteer as long as you feel like it." Specifying the duration of the commitment also tells people they still have choices; their lives and journeys are respected.

- Offer adult classes in increments people can comfortably schedule. If they sense that agreeing to a six-month study of Genesis will pressure them into committing to a six-month study of Exodus, they'll begin to do the math. (Six months times 66 books of the Bible adds up to 33 years!) It may seem there is no exit ramp.

- Train group leaders to lead through a season, a study, or a weekend teaching series. Even established group leaders need to know there's an out if they need or want one. Leaders usually have good reasons for ending their formal leadership roles: sporting schedules, job changes, travel plans, new relationships, or the healthy need to take a break to refocus on another area or stage of life. But they're often afraid of the judgment, questions, or pressure they'll face if they step away. Give them exit ramps.

Measure Every Environmental Mile Marker

I grew up in church. I grew up knowing the right answers to the right questions. I attended the services and sang the songs. I looked the part; I sounded the part; I was the part. But the part wasn't the point.

Becoming like Jesus was the point. Although I loved Jesus, the church culture was more important than the culture of the kingdom of God, and religion became my governor. So my participation in religious activities became my sole measurement of growth.

Since then, we've all learned that mere participation in church activities doesn't guarantee growth. Putting on an NFL jersey doesn't make you a football player, barking doesn't make you a dog, and attending church activities doesn't make you a Christ-follower.

So don't miss this. When we are intentional about creating environments for people to meet others who are headed the same direction (toward Christ), when we provide space for people to experience paradigm shifts in their thinking and behavior, when we invite people to connect to something bigger than themselves, we point them to Jesus and a personal relationship with him.

As a result, we still count people. Even though we can't know their motives for participating in events, classes, groups, or services, we realize that their presence matters. When we count how many people showed up in public space on a weekend, it matters. When we count the number of people who attend a retreat intended to give them space to meet with God and others, it matters. When we count the students who participate in a high school or middle school gathering, it matters. When we count the people who tithe, meet in groups, read their Bibles, or serve on a regular basis, it matters. If nothing else, counting them tells us how we're doing at creating environments that help people lean into their journey toward and with Christ.

You Can't Count It All

I have to admit it: I want to measure everything. But I can't.

- I can count every person who is in a recognized group, but I can't count everyone who shares a meaningful relationship with someone else in our church. Many people have benefited from participating in group environments that Granger has organized, while others experience informal, unorganized connection. In both cases, people are in relationships. Many people who are not in "our" groups are praying for each other, texting each other, hanging out at Starbucks together. But I don't know who they are, so I can't count them.

How often has my desire to direct and know what every person in our church is doing been driven by a need for control, a need to feel good about my performance? How about you?

- I can count every person who is serving on one of our teams, but that number doesn't include everyone who is serving. Scores of our people live out a servant lifestyle every day in their neighborhoods, their children's schools, their civic organizations, and their parachurch ministries. They're serving. But I don't know who they are.

- I can't count every Bible verse being read, every dollar being given in Jesus' name, or every relationship being invested in. I just can't know it all.

But I want to. I desperately want to.

Here's a tough question. How often has my desire to direct and know what every person in our church is doing been driven by a need for control, a need to feel good about my performance? How about you?

But It All Counts

One spring afternoon our entire staff made a short list of healthy church indicators. Our weekend attendance had been steady over several weeks and our offerings were down (perhaps due in part to an unofficial national recession), so we asked, "How do we measure health?" These expected and accurate responses went on the board:

- giving
- attendance at weekend services
- participation in groups
- volunteering
- decisions to follow Christ
- baptisms

But there was more:

- positive change, as evidenced in the lives of our people
- unstructured, informal, 24/7 servanthood in the community
- focused conversations among friends
- stories, stories, stories of next steps and life change

In our church, we measure success in two ways:

- through hard measurements: visible, identifiable, trackable numbers and percentages
- through soft measurements: feedback, stories that reveal perception, and life change.

Nothing Measures Like Story

At Granger we share stories to help us measure and celebrate the life God is breathing into our church.

- Weekly Staff Meetings—Once a week our entire staff meets for an hour to celebrate God's movement in our church and in our lives. The first third to half of every gathering is committed to "God sightings." We spontaneously share stories of life change in our people, ways God has shown up within and among our leaders, and how God is using various environments to help people move from visiting to belonging.

- Weekend Services—Our speaking pastors often include stories from the lives of our people in their messages. Occasionally we will devote an entire service to allowing people in the church to share their stories either in person or via video. In every case, these people have journeyed through church-related environments, personal relationships in and out of the church, and practices that have helped them grow closer to Jesus. Not every plot is resolved, and of course, no story is finished. But every story is a grand celebration of the grace of God.

- Social Gatherings—Retreats, affinity gatherings, Bible studies, and workshops are all ideal environments for sharing brief but profound stories of belonging and life change.

For example, during a fall weekend women's event, scores of women shared their stories. Many stories were told in private conversations, and still more were unpacked from the front of the room so everyone could celebrate.

One story was actually a collection of stories from members of a group focused on healing. They had begun their journey together as strangers, but they quickly leaned into one another, each admitting, "I haven't been able to work through this stuff on my own. I need help."

Just a few months before this women's event, one woman had filed for divorce from her second husband. A single woman was trying to sort through her confusing pattern of romantic relationships. A mother was stuck in an unhealthy pattern of relating to her adult children. A fourth woman was struggling to make her second marriage her final one.

After just a few months of sharing life in genuine, compassionate, and caring relationships, these women's story lines were developing in unexpected ways.

After just a few months of sharing life in genuine, compassionate, and caring relationships, these women's story lines were developing in unexpected ways. The first had reconciled with her husband. The single woman was beginning to see herself as God sees her: as a competent, strong adult. The mother was learning to love through offering acceptance rather than mere tolerance. The fourth woman no longer wanted to live in isolation from others.

These kinds of stories are measurements of belonging and spiritual growth. They aren't the only measurements, but they are truly critical to evaluating the church's health and gauging the effectiveness of our ministry efforts.

Celebrate Every Personal Mile Marker

If you're a full-time staff member or a volunteer leader, you likely stepped into your ministry role because you wanted to help people belong. You wanted to help introduce them to Jesus, see them develop meaningful relationships, and commit their lives to being kingdom revolutionaries.

Then ministry happened.

Meetings became more frequent. The work required to develop and stage classes, groups, training sessions, and services had no end. You found yourself moving more quickly through the church lobby. The only phone calls you seemed to make were to put out fires or respond to questions only you could answer. It's not what you signed up for.

So make the time. Recalibrate your schedule. Practice, because it won't be easy. I consciously plan to roam the hallways on the weekends so I can talk with volunteers. I read the prayer-request reports from the weekend comment cards so I can pray for our people and make phone calls.

Intentionally touching individual lives probably isn't on your calendar. It hasn't always been on mine either. In fact, secular leadership practices tell us that leaders should stay focused on leading leaders. But Jesus' approach to training his disciples was much more organic; he involved himself in the lives of babies, tax collectors, and everyone in between.

So listen for stories. Ask about people's journeys. Inquire about next steps. Find out if people are connecting. Then celebrate! Look another human being in the eye and say, "Yahoo!" (or "Praise God!"). Your affirmation will encourage your people and invigorate you.

One Final Story

Before we met her, Janet was a Christ-follower and was determined to marry someone who shared her values and beliefs. Then she met Bob. Everything about him was what she'd looked for, except that he wasn't a Christian. But he seemed sympathetic, and he accompanied her to church once in a while.

After they were married, Janet began to learn just how different Bob's values were. He thought Christians were weak, crutch-using, religious zealots who didn't live in the real world. He mocked and scoffed. When he learned that his son was dropping out of engineering school to go into youth ministry, he told him he was a fool to waste his life.

Two years in, their marriage was in trouble. Janet accepted a friend's invitation to join her at our church one weekend. She was pleased and a little amazed as she listened to a message about marriage. "Bob needs to hear this!" she thought.

Although they were not getting along and on the verge of separating, she felt almost obligated to tell Bob about the church and the current message series. He'd been uncharacteristically depressed for at least a week or more.

Before she had a chance, though, Bob had a surprising encounter with God. He'd never thought he needed God—or anyone, for that matter. He was self-made, self-sufficient. Then one weeknight as he was driving home from a trip, he realized he was lonely. It was painful, and he didn't know how to fix it. He was about to lose his second marriage. For the first time, he felt he had no control over his life.

So, for the first time in his life, he prayed.

And God met him. Bob woke up the next day, knowing something had happened. He felt clean. He felt hopeful for the first time in a long time.

He hadn't been to Granger Community Church yet, but he remembered the name. He e-mailed an urgent request to info@gccwired.com. A caring staff member called and listened.

> *I haven't been to your church yet, but I need to know what to do. My wife has left and is going to file for divorce. I have never been a Christian, and in fact, I'm embarrassed to admit that I've always made fun of Christians. Well, I was so upset last night that I prayed, "God, if there's any way that I could just get my wife to not call the attorney for one week, I might be able to convince her that I'll change." Minutes later I received a text message from my wife. It read, "Have decided to wait a week to contact an attorney. Talk to you tonight." I know God is there. I've got to do something. I already called my best friend (he and I have been merciless on Christians). I told him we had to stop. It's all changed...*

The very next day, he came to our midweek service. Then he attended the weekend service (and hasn't missed one since). The following Monday evening, Janet and Bob were in a marriage workshop, a next step from the weekend marriage series. The very next evening, he was part of a group journey and was committed to getting help from God through relationships with people.

A few months later Bob committed to following Jesus and was baptized just a couple of weeks after.

They're still on a journey. They know there are more chapters to write, more of God's story to understand, and many more lives to invest in.

Bob and Janet are home...where they belong.

From Chapter 10

Your Local Church

■ List all the on-ramps your people can access from the weekend service. If there are more than seven, consider which ones are the most viable steps for your newest guests. How will you go about reducing the number of on-ramps so that you diminish confusion and hesitation?

■ When your people take steps from the weekend service into other environments and spaces, what do the on-ramps look like from there? Are those social spaces mere collecting pools, or can strategic steps be taken from there as well?

■ What exit ramps are built into your environments? Can people step out of a group or ministry with ease, or is there a fair amount of guilt and embarrassment associated with leaving?

■ What are your hard measurements? What soft measurements are you watching? Which drives your ministry more: hard or soft measurements? Is everyone in agreement about that? What outcome are you after? Are your measurements capturing that information, or are you merely tallying activities connected to outcomes?

Your Personal Life

■ In what ways have you helped someone at your church make a connection? In what ways could you attempt to help someone connect? What could you invite someone to do? Be specific; name the person(s). Schedule it. Tap-tap. Invite someone to join you.

■ Write the story of your own steps toward and with Christ. How much of it is hard measurement, and how much is soft? When was the last time you shared this story with someone? Plan to share it with a friend this week.

Endnotes

1. Andy Stanley, Reggie Joiner, and Lane Jones, *7 Practices of Effective Ministry* (Sisters, OR: Multnomah Publishers, 2004), 94.

2. downtown.fellowshipchurch.com/thefellowshiptimes?FCW=4eq99bdk4ikct0v0meglcpk7n0.

Epilogue

What's Your Lasting Impression?

This book was written with the local church in mind. Each chapter concludes with two series of questions. The first series is focused on your church. Maybe you are in a position to influence conversation and effect change...and maybe you're not. The second set of questions is directed to you personally.

You're one person. Whether you're a pastor, a board member, a teacher, or a regular attendee, your influence matters. If people in your church are going to move from visiting to belonging, it will be primarily because of people like you. People need to know they matter. They need to know someone thinks it's a good thing they're around. They need someone to tap their shoulder and say, "Join me." Will it be you?

What you model matters. How you live matters. Here's the question: Will you practice what you hope to see new people in your church doing?

- Are you connected to other people who are helping you take steps toward Christ? To whom do you belong?

- Are you a connector of people? Does your lifestyle create an openness around you that is inclusive and inviting? Or do you send the message "That's close enough"?

- Are you still taking next steps toward becoming who and what God has designed you to be? Are you being responsible *for* yourself and *to* others?

- Are you exploring practices that deepen your intimacy with God, practices that you say you want for others in your church?

- If you told your story today, would you be able to recount recent movements of God? Would you be able to celebrate recent steps? Would you be able to talk about relationships that have made your journey what it is?

The point is not that you or I should try to be everyone's best friend. But as we spend time in public and social spaces, are we stepping outside of our group of friends to meet and encourage others who want to belong to our churches? This is a daring question for me to ask because I'm an introvert. I just happen to serve as a pastor of connections.

The lasting impressions people have of your church and mine will be made almost entirely by people. Oh sure, some will return because of the cool children's center, and others will never return because the music was too loud. But most people will come or go, stick or not stick, belong or walk away because of people. Because of you and me and the people next to us.

It's still about people. And people still matter.

Recommended Reading

Tony Morgan and Tim Stevens, *Simply Strategic Volunteers: Empowering People for Ministry.* Loveland, CO: Group Publishing, Inc., 2005.

Gary L. McIntosh, *Beyond the First Visit: The Complete Guide to Connecting Guests to Your Church.* Grand Rapids, MI: Baker Books, 2006.

Joseph R. Myers, *The Search to Belong: Rethinking Intimacy, Community and Small Groups.* El Cajon, CA: emergentYS books, 2003.

Robert D. Putnam, *Bowling Alone: The Collapse and Revival of American Community.* New York: Simon & Schuster, 2000.

Rick Warren, *The Purpose-Driven Church.* Grand Rapids, MI: Zondervan, 1995.

Bill Hybels, *The Volunteer Revolution.* Grand Rapids, MI: Zondervan, 2004.

Andy Stanley, Reggie Joiner, and Lane Jones, *7 Practices of Effective Ministry.* Sisters, OR: Multnomah Publishers, Inc., 2004.

Jim Henderson and Matt Casper, *Jim and Casper Go to Church: Frank Conversation about Faith, Churches, and Well-Meaning Christians.* Carol Stream, IL: Tyndale House Publishers, 2007.

Chuck Lawless, *Membership Matters: Insights from Effective Churches on New Member Classes and Assimilation.* Grand Rapids, MI: Zondervan, 2005.

Nelson Searcy with Jennifer Dykes Henson, *Fusion: Turning First-Time Guests into Fully-Engaged Members of Your Church.* Ventura, CA: Regal, 2007.

Chip Heath and Dan Heath, *Made to Stick: Why Some Ideas Survive and Others Die.* New York: Random House, 2007.

Henry Cloud and John Townsend, *Boundaries: When to Say Yes, When to Say No to Take Control of Your Life.* Grand Rapids, MI: Zondervan, 1992.

Andy Stanley and Bill Willits, *Creating Community: 5 Keys to Building a Small Group Culture.* Sisters, OR: Multnomah Publishers, Inc., 2004.

Tim Stevens, *Pop Goes the Church: Should the Church Engage Pop Culture?* Indianapolis, IN: Power Publishing, 2008.

Thom S. Rainer and Eric Geiger, *Simple Church.* Nashville, TN: Broadman & Holman Publishers, 2006.

John Burke, *No Perfect People Allowed: Creating a Come as You Are Culture in the Church.* Grand Rapids, MI: Zondervan, 2005.

David Kinnaman and Gabe Lyons, *unChristian: What a New Generation Really Thinks about Christianity…and Why It Matters.* Grand Rapids, MI: Baker Books, 2007.

Kem Meyer, *Less Clutter. Less Noise.: Beyond Bulletins, Brochures and Bake Sales*, Indianapolis, IN: thirty:one press, 2009.

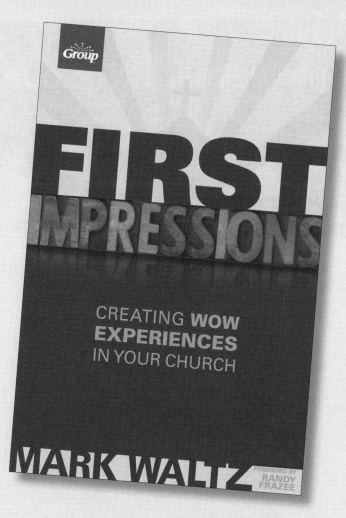

FIRST IMPRESSIONS:
Creating Wow Experiences in Your Church

By Mark Waltz

Guests in church often decide whether to return before the service has even begun. In 10 must-read chapters, this book delivers clear, relevant insights and strategies for making sure your church's first impression is its best impression. Let visitors know "You matter to God, so you matter to us."

Find this book at your favorite Christian resource provider, or go online to **group.com**.

For more amazing resources

visit us at
group.com...

...or call us at
1-800-447-1070!

Group
Incredible things will happen

NOTES

NOTES